MRS. US

IS HER TIME RUNNING OUT?

BY

ARTHUR D. WATT

ALMOND TREE PRESS

Scripture reference abbreviations used are:

KJV King James Version

NKJV New King James Version, © 1982 Thomas Nelson Publishers

NEB New English Bible, © Oxford University Press 1970

NASB New American Standard Bible, © The Lockman Foundation 1960

Mrs. Us
Is her time running out?

© 1994 by Arthur D. Watt

F   Press
5   81520

Mr. & Mrs. A. D. Watt
P.O. Box 129
Molina, CO 81646-0129

Printed in the United States of America

Ph. 970-268-5049

ISBN 0-9644645-0-0

INTRODUCTION

The last three decades of increasing crime, drug addiction, welfare costs, and teen pregnancy, along with decreasing personal freedom and scholastic achievement in the United States have clearly demonstrated that something is wrong. We see the disastrous results when a people and it's government base their values on the shifting *sands* of unproved social theories with no moral standards. America needs a change, the *right* change of turning back to God and His stabilizing standards as found in the Bible.

World famous rocket scientist, Werner von Braun, who fled from the Russians to come to the United States at the collapse of Nazi Germany, explained to the press on his arrival that he chose this country because he wanted to live and work in a land that was "based on the principles of the Bible." He had seen the disaster in his country when Hitler turned from the instructions of the Bible and tortured and murdered millions of Jews and Christians. He also knew of life and suffering in the police state of the Soviet Union where the Bible was banned. Little did he know that zealots of the secular faith of rational humanism would soon succeed in banning the Bible from our schools and start this country down the road to falling moral standards. This has now led to falling living standards. These zealots are still preaching their brand of faith in liberal humanism, but, "among scholars and scientists, however, this faith has been crumbling for some time."[1]

Over the years, I have had the opportunity of working as a scientist and engineer. In science, I saw many theories which seemed logical, and yet in time were discarded for ones quite different. As an engineer I found that it was essential to base designs not on theories, but on proven relationships.

Recently, it became apparent to me that our country, the United States, is no longer the same place of freedom that it was in years past. Three questions kept coming up in my mind: What made *us* so great? What has gone wrong with *us*? What needs to be done to fix *us*? In searching for answers to these questions, I started writing about the life and times of Mrs. Us.

This has been written from the viewpoint of an engineer who never ceases to marvel at the amazing designs produced by the Great Creator and His awesome power. I had the privilege of serving in the U.S. Navy during World War II, and later working at the National Bureau of Standards, where I learned the importance of accurate and fixed standards of reference in science and engineering. I also had the opportunity of working with many very capable engineers at the Westinghouse Electric Corporation in a number of fields of research and development.

From my experience in government, large business, and in running a small business, I have seen the importance of using proven standards. Such standards are given in the Bible. These principles and standards, espoused by many of our founding fathers and mothers were passed on to me by my loving and wise parents. These standards provide the needed stability that allows people to live and work together with the freedom God intended us to enjoy.

The framers of our Constitution were students of history and human nature. They knew how power corrupts and sought to establish a framework that would provide a government for the benefit of the people rather than for the rulers. They had seen powerful religious groups running countries for the benefit of those in power. To prevent this they wrote in Article VI that, "*Officers of the United States, and of the several states shall be bound by Oath of Affirmation to support this Constitution, but no religious test shall ever be required as a Qualification to any office.*" They also had seen how powerful kings and ruling parties had taken away the right of individuals to *worship God as they saw fit.* To prevent this, they wrote in the First Amendment, "*Congress shall make no law respecting an establishment of religion, or prohibiting the free exercise thereof; or abridging the freedom of speech,….*" Those who penned the constitution knew full well that it would work for a people that valued freedom more than life itself and who had God's moral law written in their hearts.

God has left each individual free to choose to read or not to read His Word. The U.S. Constitution, as written, provides the citizens of our country this same freedom of choice. In the 1960s, the courts, manipulated by a few social theorists, started to remove this freedom with the aid of a mythical "separation of church and state" quote which is not in our Constitution. Sometimes they used a vague reference to an "establishment clause". Congress has retained its constitutional right to open with prayer. It seems only fair that our citizens, including our school children, should have their same constitutional freedom of choice to pray or read God's Word wherever and whenever they choose.

In the 1960s President Johnson initiated the war on poverty. Today, some 30 years later, we have more people on welfare and in real moral poverty than when this program started. Providing for the "right to not work" has contributed to an alarming burden of illegitimacy which has soared to as high as 80% in some regions of our country.[2] Now we are starting to reap the bitter fruit of both moral decay and a rising financial burden.

The "war on poverty" and the "war on drugs" failed because those running the programs failed to identify the real enemy and started attacking the symptoms. Now Congress and the President are starting the "war on crime." Will it, like the previous programs, suffer from the belief in Washington that any problem can be solved by spending more money? Giving money to people who are able to work destroys their incentive to work. It leaves them with time on their hands which can lead to boredom. The extra time and money often leads them to turn to alcohol, sex, drugs, and then to crime to support their addictions. Good, productive, and interesting work helps make helpful, happy, and useful citizens, but the most powerful force in producing law-abiding citizens is having God's moral law written in their hearts. Although some are proposing a strong federal police force to control crime, this raises the risk of loss of personal freedom. We must be careful not to repeat what happened in Stalin's Russia with the KGB or Hitler's Germany with the Gestapo. The real answer for America is to turn back to God!

The following chapters describe the life and times of Mrs. Us, her current problems, how she got into them, and ways to solve them. Read about the encounters of Mrs. Us with her doctors in Washington and listen to the advice of her friends, Dr. Truth, Nurse Trustworthy, Sonny, the Watcher, and Mother Earth. They tell her about the past as well as the future. They describe her ailments, the real pollution problems, what went wrong in the 1960s, and what needs to be done to help her regain her former health. They also warn her of what may happen if the right changes are not made now.

You and I can help Mrs. Us regain her former health, and as citizens of her land have a responsibility to do this. Almost 3,000 years ago the prophet Elijah was sent with a message to a nation in decay. Many were sitting idly by while the activist prophets of Baal were leading the nation in worshipping the false gods of sensual self-gratification. Elijah stepped forward and said to the people, *"How long will you sit on the fence? If the Lord is God, follow Him; but if Baal, then follow him."* [3] If enough of us get off the fence and really follow God, it can again be said, *"They helped every one his neighbor; and everyone said to his brother, Be of good courage."* [4]

---

[1] Dennis Farney, Natural Questions, "Pride and Secular Humanism," *The Wall Street Journal,* July 11, 1994.

[2] Charles Krauthammer "The Scourge of Illegitimacy-Stop the Subsidy," *Readers Digest,* March 1994,pp49-53

[3] I Kings 18:21, NEB

[4] Isaiah 41:6, KJV

ACKNOWLEDGMENTS

Thanks are due to my loving wife Ann, and to my dear friends: Charles Smith, Dee MacNeil, Art Farstad, Don Chittick, Ann Stringer, Jim Terry, Norm Frank, Chris Lange, Don and Inez Petersen, and Anne Wulff, who along with others have provided much needed help and encouragement during the writing of this book.

Don Watt 9/8/94

CONTENTS

CHAPTER 1

MRS. US IS ILL

Searching for the Right Rx

Mrs. Us has been ill for some time, and even now as she gazes out across the harbor, her right arm seems heavy, and there appears to be a tear in her eye. In 1992 she was diagnosed as needing a change, as well she might. She even knew that herself, but didn't seem to know what change to try. Before the elections the evening news reported her condition as very grim. A day or so after the elections, Mrs. Us was assured over TV that some of her charts had apparently been misread and that she was actually in pretty good shape. In spite of this news, Mrs. Us really didn't feel better; she still had her arthritis and a pain near her heart. Yesterday as she tried to stoop down and welcome a new arrival to the Land of the Free, she almost choked on the word *freedom*—was it really still here, she wondered to herself?

For quite a few years, her doctors in her capital city, at both ends of Pennsylvania Avenue, and the nine specialists in black robes had been trying various treatments. Some helped for a day or so, but often she got downright worse. Much of the time her doctors did not agree on the cause of her pain and often offered quite different medicine to try to ease her symptoms. Mrs. Us was beginning to wonder if her doctors were really looking for the cause of her illness or were they just prescribing pain killers? After the 1992 election was over, she started to cheer up. "Maybe now that all my doctors are from the same medical school they will agree on a treatment." Soon that old uneasy feeling returned. She began to wonder, "Now they may all agree and give me major surgery that I don't really need, and I'll get worse."

Mrs. Us, who was in the hospital for more tests, decided to ring for Nurse Trustworthy. For some reason Nurse Trustworthy, with her cheery smile, always made Mrs. Us feel better. "You know," she thought, "my doctors are so busy planning what's best for their medical schools that they haven't time to think about what is best for me."

Just then Nurse Trustworthy walked in with a cheery "Good morning."

Mrs. Us was feeling better already as she whispered to her nurse, "Please, my dear, could you get a copy of my medical history and read it to me? My doctors are so busy, and I'm not always sure if they are really telling me the whole truth about my condition."

Nurse Trustworthy was soon back from the record room and, closing the door, she started to read…

MEDICAL HISTORY

"Born 1787 in Philadelphia, Pennsylvania. Attending physicians: the Founding Fathers, including George Washington, James Madison, and many other brilliant God-fearing men. You know," the nurse added, "they wrote your birth certificate, the CONSTITUTION OF THE UNITED STATES."

Mrs. Us was feeling better as she listened to the Preamble of her Constitution: "*We the people of the United States, in Order to form a more perfect Union, establish Justice, insure domestic Tranquillity, provide for the common defence, promote the general Welfare, and secure the Blessings of Liberty to ourselves and our Posterity, do ordain and establish this Constitution of the United States of America.*"

A smile flitted across her face as her mind drifted back to the dedicated men who labored through the hot Philadelphia summer to write this document. She could almost hear James Madison as he declared, "*We have staked the future of all of our political institutions upon the capacity of mankind for self-government; upon the capacity of each and all of us to govern ourselves, to control ourselves, to sustain ourselves accord-*

ing to the Ten Commandments of God."[1] Her mind then drifted to George Washington as she could hear him say, *"Just government protects all in their religious rights, true religion affords to government its surest support."* And, *"It is impossible to rightly govern ... without God and the Bible."*[2] Then Mrs. Us quietly dozed off for a moment.

She awoke with a start as she mused out loud, "Maybe a look at my history is really helping. I would like to share some of this with my school children."

Nurse Trustworthy broke in, "Mrs. Us, I'm not sure your lawyers would let you tell this to your school children. You know how hung up they are on this *separation of church and state* kick. You and I know it's not in your Constitution, but most of your school children and many of your lawyers believe it is," she said with a sigh, and then left the room.

At this point Mrs. Us reached for the papers the nurse had left. She started to read the First Amendment over again, *"Congress shall make no law respecting an establishment of religion, or prohibiting the free exercise thereof; or abridging the freedom of speech, or of the press; or the right of the people peaceably to assemble, and to petition the Government for a redress of grievances."*

"Sounds clear enough to me," she said to herself with a smile. "My children should be free to pray or read the Bible wherever and whenever they wish."

The smile on her face faded as Mrs. Us's mind drifted back to the days of slavery when not all men were considered as having equal rights to the "Blessings of Liberty." A frown crossed her brow as she remembered the traumatic and painful days of the Civil War. Tears came to her eyes as she recalled the death and suffering of so many of her sons and daughters, and the gross injustice brought on by war. She thought of the heartaches President Lincoln must have had as he struggled with a nation at war with itself and how he often turned to his Bible for help.[3]

Her face softened as her thoughts turned to George Washington Carver. Born at the end of this conflict, the son of slaves, he rose above his surroundings. With encouragement from his parents' former master, he went on to contribute greatly to his country, and his people. For his many contributions, this humble man received many national and international honors.

Mrs. Us's thoughts then jumped to more recent times to a man who had a dream of equality for all such as the Founding Fathers had envisioned. Martin Luther King was a man with a vision. Although he did not live to see the fruit of his efforts, he and many others helped bring about much-needed change. The smile on her face again faded as she thought of the present plight of so many of her dear children of many races and colors growing up without someone to teach them the way to true joy and inner peace that God is offering them. "I wish," she thought, "there were more of my parents and teachers who would challenge my children to become happy and productive members of my family. If only they could be challenged by the Bible message, '*But be doers of the word, and not hearers only, deceiving yourselves.*'[4] Then they would have the joy of learning, producing, and giving." She paused as she mused on the tremendous strides in scientific knowledge that have been made in the last half century. "What endless possibilities for a great and enjoyable life for all my children," she thought.

A sharp pain in her heart reminded her of the need to continue searching for a cure to her immediate ailments. Mrs. Us rang for her nurse and asked to see the charts of her progress over the years.

CHARTS

Mrs. Us had by and large enjoyed a healthy life with some of the normal ups and downs. She grew rapidly at an early age, and her health was the envy of all her friends and neighbors. The Founding Fathers saw to it that her children were taught the difference between right and wrong in her schools. Their books were full of the lessons found in the Bible that are so essential to the health of a self- governing society. These Founding Fathers were well aware of the inherent selfishness of man, and how power can corrupt. To guard against this, they produced a phenomenal blueprint in the U.S. Constitution with three independent sources of power, each with it's own sphere of responsibilities and authority. "This may be part of my problem," she said to herself, "*selfishness and corruption.*" Then she reached for the first chart the nurse was showing her.

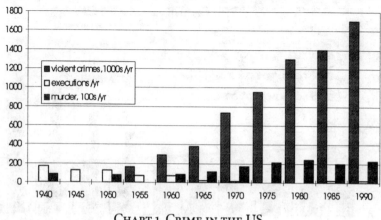

CHART 1. CRIME IN THE US

Mrs. Us was taken aback at the phenomenal growth in violent crime over the past thirty years. Her heart began to ache again as she thought of the death and suffering of so many of her children. "What went wrong in the late 50s and early 60s?" she mused out loud.

Nurse Trustworthy broke in, "I think that's when your nine specialists in the building with the tall marble columns across the street from Capitol Hill gave you a new prescription. They thought it would be better for you if your children didn't pray or read the Bible in your public schools. The new medicine, sort of like the old Bible burning, had something on the label about the need to remove the old outdated thoughts of boundaries on behavior and of right and wrong."

Mrs. Us mused, "I think that the fine print read *separation of church and state*. It surely tasted bad and I almost gagged, but they made me force it down."

The nurse now handed Mrs. Us her second chart. There was silence for a few moments as she examined it. Then she sobbed, "Look at all my dear young boys and girls in prison. What a waste. Why did the rapid increase in crime start in the mid 70s?"

Her nurse answered, "That's because it took about 10 years for young children growing up with no knowledge of God and His Word, and His boundaries of right and wrong, to become violent repeat criminals."

Looking closer, Mrs. Us exclaimed, "And look at all those lawyers!

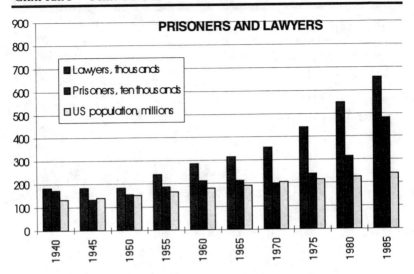

CHART 2. PRISONERS AND LAWYERS

With their astronomical fees they must be costing me a pretty penny! Old George Washington must have been right; self government won't work without God and the Bible."

Hoping to find better news in the next chart, Mrs. Us asked, "How

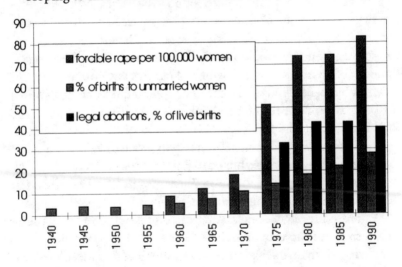

CHART 3. CHANGES FOR WOMEN IN THE US

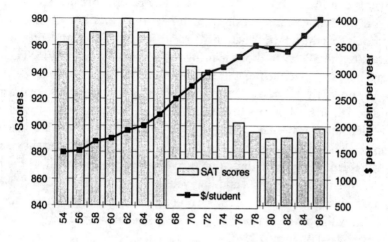

CHART4. SAT SCORES AND STUDENT EXPENSES

are my daughters faring?"

The nurse handed her Chart 3, and said in a whisper, "Not very well, not very well."

Mrs. Us gasped as she looked at the number of rapes. "Where have all my clean-cut young men gone who would protect a girl from danger instead of putting her through the traumatic and humiliating experience of rape? Look at all those young girls who have become pregnant (by males, not real men) and have been left to struggle with raising children by themselves. Even worse, many were forced to go through the short and long term trauma of abortion."

Nurse Trustworthy exclaimed, "You know that your schools were instructed to teach sex, sometimes starting in kindergarten. It looks like they learned how to do sex, but not when *not* to do it!"

"Let's look at the schools," Mrs. Us said, hoping for better news. The nurse showed her Chart 4. "Something really went wrong in the early 60s!" she exclaimed. "Things started to look better in the 80s. Maybe we finally spent our way out of the hole."

"Not quite," Nurse Trustworthy injected. "As you can see from 1960 to 1980 the spending per student more than doubled even as the SAT scores continued to drop. In the 70s many parents became so fed up with the crime, guns, condoms, and new doctrines taught in many schools that they started their own private schools. These students went back to the *3Rs* instead of majoring in sex and self-expression. Their much better scores helped raise the over-all average."

By now Mrs. Us was exhausted from looking at charts and said to her nurse, "My dear, I'm very tired now. Are there many more?"

Her nurse answered, "Yes, Mrs. Us, I'm afraid that there are many more charts that you should see, but since you are tired, we will skip over them. They show that your workers have to spend half of their working time to pay taxes and that your welfare and health costs have gotten out of hand. Let me show you one last chart and then we must get on with your diagnosis." With that, the nurse handed her Chart 5: her personal finances.

"Oh my!," Mrs. Us exclaimed, "My doctors on the Hill don't seem to know how to balance my books." Nurse Trustworthy started to say something about her other charts, when Mrs. Us blurted out, "I know, I know, that's when my children who grew up without any boundaries started to become violent, to go to jail, to become activists instead of workers. Then I had to pay for all the lawyers, crime and drug fighters, jailers, welfare recipients, the crooked bankers, and the AIDS patients."

Mrs. Us fell back in her bed, and looking up at Nurse Trustworthy, she asked, "Nurse, am I terminal?"

"I'm your nurse, not your doctor!" Nurse Trustworthy exclaimed. "I have some other patients who are needing me, so I must go, but I'll send in Dr. Truth to make a diagnosis and give you a prescription. Your new doctor at 1600 Pennsylvania Avenue has a nice bedside manner, but until we know a little more about his medicine, you better have a session with Dr. Truth. You know," she added, "I was the nurse at your birth. Most of your attending physicians had a well-worn medical book on their desk. They called it *The Book*. It had answers for all kinds of ailments, especially for those like yours. They had to read and study it to get to the truth. It contains lots of good reading and has helped many of my patients."

Nurse Trustworthy leaned over her patient and said softly, "Your doc-

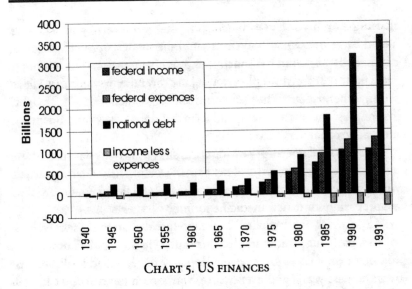

CHART 5. US FINANCES

tors probably wouldn't believe this, but most of them had a kind of cellular phone link to a consulting physician. Worked fine for most—they didn't even have a monthly or user fee. There were no busy signals either, but it seemed to work best when they were on their knees. The One on the other end of the line really helped when needed. Your Founding Fathers knew Him by several names. Some called Him the Great Physician, others the Almighty, and some the Creator (not too popular with some these days), and then there were those who knew Him well and called Him Father." With this, Nurse Trustworthy leaned over and kissed Mrs. Us on the cheek, and whispered, "God bless you, my dear; get well!" And then she was gone.

DOCTOR'S VISIT

Within moments Dr. Truth appeared. He only glanced toward the charts because it seems he already knew what was on them. With a kindly, "Good morning, Mrs. Us," he firmly grasped her by the hand and peered into her eyes. He then whipped out a well-worn stethoscope that had been used on a good many patients like Mrs. Us. Listening carefully for a few moments, he straightened up and said, "You have a heart problem that must be fixed. If not done soon, you will be terminal." Then he added, "You are also suffering from a number of other problems: crime, drugs, high taxes, and too much spending. Before we can fix them, we must first take care of your heart. You have several symptoms that I have seen in other patients who were terminal: high violent crime, high debt, loss of jobs, and yes, the same old terminal signs of sex out of control, rape, and sexual perversion."

This news did not surprise Mrs. Us, as she recalled the data presented in her charts and the severity of her pains. "Doctor," she said in a guarded voice, "I have been told that my doctors at 1600 Pennsylvania Avenue are preparing some new medicine for me."

"I know," Dr. Truth replied, "I used to be called in to those meetings in years past, but I wasn't invited this time." He then looked down and said in a firm voice, "You have developed some very bad health habits over the past years, and even worse, you took a large dose of liberal drugs that almost finished you off. You really need some very strong medicine which you may not want to take. To help you make the right decision, I'll have your nurse stop by with someone from the Central Records Department to give you a clearer picture of your condition and need for treatment."

MORE RECORDS

Nurse Trustworthy came in early the next day with a white-robed messenger carrying a large record book that had "US" on the cover. After a brief "Good morning, Mrs. Us," the nurse took the book and started to read: "Each year since your birth, you have been sent a number of living souls to care for on temporary loan. Some arrived by sea, some by land, and recently some by air. Oh, yes, each year many arrived by womb. With each soul came a very special Gift box placed in layaway until claimed. In years past, as prescribed in your birth certificate, you provided most, but not all of them with the blessings of liberty and the common defense. You were also given an Instruction Book which in your younger years you provided to almost every new arrival. This Book contained instructions for the care and raising of your children. It set up boundaries for their protection, and yes, it tells how to claim and open the Gift box."

In an unusually stern voice, Nurse Trustworthy read on, "You didn't always heed the Instruction Book given you. Some of your sons and daughters were enslaved, beaten, and mistreated. You did not provide liberty to all, and from 1861 to 1865 your sons fought each other, and some 600,000 lives were lost and many others maimed and wounded. In spite of this, compared to many of your sister countries, you did provide a land of opportunity for most souls placed in your care. You also are commended for the way you have responded to those in need throughout the world. Like all your sisters, you have had your ups and downs. For a number of generations, you passed on from parents to children the important boundaries and guidelines essential to living in a free country.

"Over the years you also passed on to many of your children the essential information on how to claim their Gift box." Nurse Trustworthy looked up from her reading. "You know," she said, "there is some bad news, and yes, some good news about the souls sent to you. They all were created with the right to choose between good and bad. The first production model made a bad choice and suffered a fall. This damaged an essential gene. I think it was part of the life-extending and immune system, which has shown up on all models since then. The good news is that the Designers knew this was coming, so They designed a retrofit implant kit to correct the defect. This implant kit was very costly to the manufacturer. In fact, the Chief Designer had to die to make it available. Amazing as it may seem, this implant kit contained in every Gift box is offered free to every living soul. Like most gifts, it only becomes effective for those who choose to receive it. This kit provides, among other things, a new heart. When properly maintained by daily reading from the Book, this implant kit produces a person who loves his God and his neighbor as himself. This makes for a good citizen in a land of freedom. Fortunately, in your early days this Gift from God, called *eternal life*, was claimed by many of your sons and daughters.

"Now I must read on since this record book is out on overnight loan." Her eyes dropped to the book and she continued reading. "'After World War II, many of your parents concentrated on making money, having the good life, and pursuing the ever-elusive happiness. Many who were sent to tell you the message about the Gift became so busy with new buildings and social programs that they did not notice that more and more of the Gift boxes were being returned unclaimed. This pleased Arch-Enemy, alias Father of Lies, alias the Deceiver, who hates freedom and tries to hide information about the Gift. Early in the 60s he saw an opportunity to start removing your freedom. He quietly slipped a few activist lawyers into the building with the tall marble columns to argue before the nine specialists in black robes. These lawyers, in the guise of liberty, persuaded the specialists to take away the freedom of your children to pray or have a Bible in school. The busy parents did not seem to notice, and even worse, forgot the directions to teach their children right from wrong and to study and learn from the Book. Soon children were having children who did not know right from wrong. In fact, some of their teachers were telling them there *was* no right or wrong.'"

Looking up, Nurse Trustworthy said, "You may wonder how they did it so easily. For a number of years, Arch Enemy had been recruiting assistants. He had learned from his successes in Nazi Germany that if you tell a lie often enough, soon it will be believed. Arch Enemy required each of his recruits to repeat five times every day, 'I evolved— there is no God.' Soon he had quite a following. It seems that many of the highly educated learned this incantation quickly. Now he had to find a way to get the right specialists into the building with the tall marble columns. Soon he found help from some of your doctors on the Hill. Dr. Big Talk was one who helped lead the inquisitions held each time a new specialist was to be appointed. Their mission was to prevent anyone who had not learned the new interpretive medicine from being confirmed. Often they were quite successful, and then you know the rest."

Turning back to the record book, the nurse continued reading. "'Starting in the 70s something alarming, called *choice*, happened. We started receiving back from you millions of unclaimed soul packages stamped RETURN TO SENDER—NOT WANTED.'" Nurse Trustworthy paused to catch her breath. "I'm sure this made the Sender unhappy. Sure seems strange that snuffing out a life should be called *choice*, when that word used to mean *the very best*. I can't get used to your new words. Why are persons who die at about half or less the average life span, commit so many suicides, and are three times more likely to become alcoholics called *gay*?"

With a sigh, Nurse Trustworthy said, "Now for some good news," and began to read. "'In 1990, at the urging of some dedicated Christian lawyers opposing Arch Enemy, your nine specialists made a decision allowing Christian Clubs (Prayer Clubs, Bible Clubs, etc.) the right to function on public school campuses. Unfortunately two to three years later, with the aid of Arch Enemy, many schools don't seem to know about this recent ruling.'" At this point the white-robed messenger's beeper went off and he and the record book seemed to vanish.

Placing her hand on Mrs. Us's forehead, Nurse Trustworthy said in her usual caring voice, "I'm sorry to have read so much, but Dr. Truth wanted me to let you know what led up to your present condition. You know, he went to consult with the Great Physician, and should be back soon." She brushed back a few wrinkled hairs, and with a soft "Good night" was gone.

DOCTOR'S SECOND VISIT

The next morning Mrs. Us awoke to see Dr. Truth standing over her with a file folder under one arm. Getting right to the point, the doctor said, "I have just come back from the consulting office of *Father, Son, and Holy Spirit*. Some think of it as a Law office, as it is in a way, but really they serve as Physician, Designer, Builder, Judge, Chief Ruler, and yes, Comforter. They confirmed my diagnosis—you have a heart problem, and they are in general agreement with my prescriptions. After I give you these, I'll also give you a copy of the consultant's report. Since your problem has been going on for more than a generation, the normal preventive medicine won't be enough. It will take strong medicine to turn back the violence and crime. What made you great, Mrs. Us, was *trust* based on *truth*. Your founders trusted God, and could be trusted by their neighbors. Trust can only be restored when men become trustworthy, men of integrity and character. A person who has been raised to lie, steal, and hate is almost impossible to change except when given a new heart from his Gift kit." The doctor then began to scribble on his pad, and tearing off four sheets, each with a big Rx on the corner, he handed them to Mrs. Us.

PRESCRIPTIONS

Rx 1—*Turn from sin.* God is sending you messengers. You will know them, they are the ones who both tell and do God's Word. They will speak to your Christians who have become complacent in loving worldly things and are not loving God with all their heart and soul and mind. They will tell them that they must ask God to forgive them, turn from sin in their life and place His will above all else. Then they must tell all their friends and neighbors how to find their Free Gift from God.

Rx 2—*Turn to God.* He is sending you messengers. They will tell your sons and daughters how to claim the Gift and make it theirs. The heart-changing power of this retrofit kit has been proven effective over the centuries since the Chief Designer paid for it by His death, and proved its power by His resurrection. This is the only hope to reach your children who have been raised without the knowledge of God and boundaries of right and wrong. With new hearts, you can be sure your crime rate will drop quickly.

Rx 3—*Turn from bondage.* You have lost much of your early freedom. Arch Enemy has made many of your sons and daughters slaves—slaves to drugs, alcohol, tobacco, pornography, and perverted sex. Addictions are hard to break, but the retrofit kit, when properly maintained, has the power to free your sons and daughters. You should, however, make every effort to keep your young children from the pain of these addictions. Mothers and fathers, if those inspired by Arch Enemy have taken over your schools, *take them back*!

You also have become slaves of big government. This is a creeping disease. First you think you are getting something *free* from government. Then you become *dependent* upon government, only to awaken and find you are *slaves* of government. *Take back your government!* Let it once again become your servant rather than you its slave.

Rx 4—*Turn to work.* Too many persons in Washington and elsewhere in government are drawing huge salaries sitting around talking and planning more ways to increase your taxes. The Washington brokerage charge has become too large. Your companies, Mrs. Us, are so burdened down with taxes, regulations, legal fees, and health insurance that it is hard for them to function, let alone compete in a global market. Take this message to your doctors on the Hill and at 1600 Pennsylvania Avenue.

Let my people go! Go back to work at productive, creative jobs, freed from excessive regulation and tax burdens. Provide your companies with a safe, stable and truthful environment. Eliminate the shifting sand traps on the business course set up by a big government that keeps changing the rules and always wants more taxes, and never says *enough*. With a safe, stable, and fair environment, businesses will provide jobs for all your children.

Dr. Truth grasped Mrs. Us's hand in both of his, and looking her straight in the eye, he said, "This medicine, will work if you take it." Then in a stern voice he said, "Twenty-five years ago, General Harold K. Johnson, Chief of Staff of your Army gave you a prescription, '*Turn to God*.'[5] You did not listen to him. Instead you took more of the tranquilizers Arch-Enemy had his doctors prescribe for you. Now they are prescribing pep pills and liberal drug therapy. If you make the wrong choice

27

again, you don't have long to live." Then handing her the consultant's report he said, "*Choose carefully and quickly, Mrs. Us.*" And then he was gone.

CONSULTANT'S REPORT

MEMORANDUM

FROM:	THE GREAT PHYSICIAN
TO:	DR. TRUTH
REFERENCE:	MRS. US

YOUR DIAGNOSIS OF A HEART PROBLEM IS CORRECT. HERE ARE THREE CHOICES, OFTEN OVERLOOKED, THAT MAY HELP YOU IN YOUR PRESCRIPTIONS:

1 - I CALL HEAVEN AND EARTH TO RECORD THIS DAY AGAINST YOU, THAT I HAVE SET BEFORE YOU LIFE AND DEATH, BLESSING AND CURSING: THEREFORE CHOOSE LIFE THAT BOTH THOU AND THY SEED MAY LIVE.[6]

2 - IF MY PEOPLE WHICH ARE CALLED BY MY NAME, SHALL HUMBLE THEMSELVES, AND PRAY, AND SEEK MY FACE, AND TURN FROM THEIR WICKED WAYS, THEN WILL I HEAR FROM HEAVEN, AND FORGIVE THEIR SIN, AND WILL HEAL THEIR LAND.[7]

3 - FOR THE WAGES OF SIN IS DEATH, BUT THE GIFT OF GOD IS ETERNAL LIFE IN CHRIST JESUS OUR LORD.[8]

URGE YOUR PATIENT TO CHOOSE LIFE, HUMBLE HERSELF, AND URGE HER CITIZENS TO PICK UP THEIR GIFT PACKAGES.

CHAPTER NOTES

My friend, remember that *we* are Mrs. Us. There are very few nations that God has blessed as much as the U.S. He also takes nations as well as individuals to the woodshed and sometimes destroys them when they turn from Him. The pages of history are full of nations that God has disciplined and those that He has had to destroy. It is clear from Mrs. Us's charts that we are in serious trouble. I do not know if enough of Us will repent in time to escape self-destruction, or God's judgment.

I *do* know that He will receive you *as an individual* if you come to Him and claim your special Gift of God. When you do, He will put real meaning into your life, and spare you from the wrath of judgment to come. God's message to individual and nation alike is, "*Come to Me, all you who labor and are heavy laden, and I will give you rest.*"[9] Let those of us who know and enjoy this rest bring the message of God's love to our friends and neighbors.

President Clinton reminded us in his inaugural address from Galatians 6:19 of the importance of reaping. In the preceding verses, God reminds us all of the importance of sowing, "Do not be *deceived, God is not mocked: for whatever a man sows, that will he also reap. For he who sows to his flesh will of the flesh reap corruption, but he who sows to the Spirit will of the Spirit reap everlasting life.*"[10]

We all know that Mrs. Us is reaping a harvest of increasing crime, violence, ill health, and loss of financial strength. If we and our nation's leaders really *turn to God* and start sowing the right seed, crime will decrease, productive jobs will increase, health care costs will drop, and the deficit can be brought under control.

If instead we turn further away from God, His message to us may well be that from the prophet Hosea: "*For they have sown the wind, and they shall reap the whirlwind;*" and later in the chapter, "*I will send a fire upon his cities, and it shall devour the palaces thereof.*"[11] Last year we saw two devastating wind storms and one fire storm in our cities. They cost the nation billions of dollars at a time we can ill afford it. God is trying to get our attention. Let's do our part to help Mrs. Us recover.[12]

29

[1] James Madison, *The Papers of James Madison*, June 20, 1785. See also David Barton, *The Myth of Separation*, WallBuilders Press, Aledo, TX , 1992.

[2] Washington, *The Writings of Washington*, Vol. XXX, May 10, 1789

[3] Gerald Parshall, "Who Was Lincoln", *U.S. News and World Report*, Oct. 5, 1992

[4] James 1:22, NKJV

[5] *US News and World Report*, Feb. 12, 1968

[6] Deuteronomy 30:19, KJV

[7] II Chronicles 7:14, KJV

[8] Romans 6:23, NKJV

[9] Matthew 11:28 NKJV

[10] Galations 6:7&8 NKJV

[11] Hosea 8:7,&14 KJV

[12] I am indebted to David Barton of the WallBuilders, for the material in Chart 4. His excellent books and lectures encouraged me to write this chapter. The data for the other charts is from the *Statistical Abstracts of the United States*.

CHAPTER 2

MRS. US'S MELTING POT

USING THE RIGHT FLUX

MRS. US WAS TIRED FROM HER STAY AT THE HOSPITAL. SHE PAUSED FOR BREATH BEFORE CLIMBING THE STAIRS TO HER VANTAGE POINT LOOKING OUT OVER THE HARBOR. HER PURSE was bulging with old medicine bottles received from her doctors in Washington, and yes, the four unfilled prescriptions just received from Dr. Truth. She looked up and started to read, "Give me your tired, your poor…." Her mind flashed back to the charts showing the surge of violence and crime in her cities. Will they really be better off here, she wondered? Her mind then turned to the TV news she had watched while in the hospital. How sad to see the pain and anguish as men fight each other in Bosnia, Africa, Asia, and yes, here in America. She knew that this had been going on as far back as recorded history, but here in America, things were supposed to be better. "I know they used to be," she said out loud. "Yes, we had our problems, but much of the time my melting pot used to work. That's it!" she exclaimed. "My melting pot needs fixing!"

Since she didn't feel like climbing the stairs anyway, she decided to stop at the phone booth and call her friend. The cheery, "Good afternoon, this is Nurse Trustworthy," from the other end of the line made her feel better.

Then she said, "This is Mrs. Us. I think that my melting pot needs fixing. Do you know if any of my doctors on the Hill or at 1600 Pennsylvania Avenue are good at fixing melting pots?"

There was a moment of silence before the nurse replied. "Mrs. Us, most of your doctors at these locations are lawyers. They have been tinkering with your melting pot for quite a while, but I don't think they are the ones you need. They repainted it, and yes, pasted lots of new laws on it, but it didn't do much good. Even now they are working on some new anti-hate signs and gun controls. What your melting pot really needs is some internal fixing, and some new flux. You had better call Doctor Wisdom's office. They have some engineers and metallurgists who I'm sure can help and, oh yes, if you can find an old-time farmer, check with him. You know those old farmers were a self-reliant lot. They could fix almost anything."

Mrs. Us thanked her nurse, and was about to hang up when Nurse Trustworthy asked, "Mrs. Us, have you taken the medicine Dr. Truth prescribed for you?"

Mrs. Us replied, "I have been so busy that I haven't even been to the pharmacy. My doctors on the Hill and at 1600 Pennsylvania Avenue usually gave me the medicine or a shot right in their office without even asking me if I wanted it. Some of those shots really hurt and gave me an allergic reaction."

"Dr. Truth is different," the nurse replied, "He always tells you what is best, but then He lets you choose. Mrs. Us, you are almost as bad as my nine-year old at home. He really puts things off, and sometimes I have to tell him, 'Take your medicine like a man.' Whoops, now we have to say 'like a person.' Mrs. Us, so you won't put this off I'll call Dr. Wisdom's office and have them send out an engineer to check over your melting pot. Now, my dear, you had better climb up your stairs, get a good night's sleep, and wait for the engineer who will be there first thing tomorrow morning."

SONNY'S VISIT

Early the next morning, Mrs. Us looked out and saw a small boat pull up to her island. Going to the door, she was surprised to see a young man in a white lab jacket jump onto the dock with a tool kit and a large bag marked *The Right Flux.*.

"Good morning Mrs. Us. My name is Sonny" he said politely, "I've come to work on your melting pot."

Mrs. Us replied, "Sonny, have you worked on melting pots before? You look a bit young to me."

"I know," Sonny replied, "I really do have a degree in fixing melting pots, and have helped fix quite a few. Since yours is so large, before headquarters would let me see you, they insisted that I stop and see an old farmer for some advice. Come to find out, he was a tall, lanky fellow with a sad but kind face. He told me that he knew you years ago and that he even lived at 1600 Pennsylvania Avenue for a short time. Asked me to pass on his greetings and was sorry to hear that you were ill and that your melting pot needed fixing again. Seems he had a hard time trying to fix it when he was with you.

"You know, Mrs. Us, that melting pots need careful adjustment. The temperature must be just right, and they require careful stirring. Not too slow or they will stick, or too fast, as they will spill over and cause a real mess. I was also warned that Arch Enemy often slips in and turns up the heat. This makes it a boiling pot and when it flashes over, things get real bad. He likes to throw in some bad flux that causes separation instead of a nice blend. He keeps telling people that they have a right to be angry and that they need special rights for their own group.

"When I talked to the old farmer, he said to be sure to remind you that according to your Constitution, all in your melting pot have equal rights to freedom, and protection under just and uniform laws. Seems he knew a lot about law. He told me that special laws for self-interest groups can really mess up melting pots. He said to look out for quotas as sometimes they put undesired lumps in the melting- pot mixtures." With this, Sonny said, "I'm sorry to have kept you standing so long. Can we go upstairs and look at your recent melting pot records? Then I must look at your melting pot and see what is needed to fix it. I'll also leave you this bag of *The Right Flux* and a page of instructions for the successful operation of melting pots."

MELTING POT RECORDS

Sonny noticed that the records started in 1776, with minor problems cropping up from time to time. He saw that the melting pot grew rapidly in size, and by 1836 some serious divisions over slavery started to erupt. In 1837 there was a financial panic, and in 1861 the pot went critical and almost split in two. Flipping over to more recent times, he noticed some serious problems in the 1960s. The temperature started to rise in the late 1950s, and by 1962 serious separations were seen in the melting pot. The Supreme Court got involved in social tinkering, which some called social engineering. When Sonny saw the words *social engineering*, he got upset since he knew that engineers worked with proven physical laws rather than with guesses and unproved theories. He also noted that about this time the flux additions, which were used to promote good mixing, almost stopped. Sonny wondered if Arch Enemy had turned up the heat and had started adding some new flux of his own.

He saw that Mrs. Us became involved in Viet Nam, a war she lost and that cost her many lives. He saw next that riots began to break out with fire storms in the cities. Schools were becoming battle grounds instead of learning grounds. Mrs. Us heard Sonny groan as he read the list of cities with racial strife and fire storms. He also noted that there was a large influx of Latin Americans and Asians into the melting pot that seemed to remain as unassimilated lumps. Closing the record book he turned and said, "Let's go down and look at your melting pot."

When they entered the melting-pot room, it was really a mess. No one seemed to be at the controls and people were running around with new additives they poured in from time to time. In addition, the floor was a mess where the pot had boiled over.

"Mrs. Us, you really need to watch your melting pot more carefully," Sonny said sternly. "You need to set a watch on the temperature and stirrer controls." Looking over at the melting pot, they saw some activists, who thought they knew melting pots, trying new flux combinations. Sonny saw a bag labeled *New Morality*. He opened it a bit, then quickly closed it. "Smells like the *Old Immorality* to me!" he exclaimed. "We almost always find this around melting pots that have gone into final failure." Then he turned to a bag labeled *New Liberty*. Looking inside, he saw the instructions: If you like it—do it; don't discriminate—anything is OK. Taking a sniff, he said "They must have put in some cheap perfume to try to cover up the real smell." Then he saw a bag labeled *New Parenting*. Looking at the fine print he saw the following: Let them have their own way; if you are busy, just forget the kids—social services will take over. To one side they saw a nice-looking big bag labeled *Change*. "About time for a change," Sonny said, as he walked over to take a closer look. The workers were pouring material from several containers into this bag. Most seemed to be coming from a container whose label had just fallen to the floor. Sonny picked up the label and groaned as he read: "MORE TAXES—WE HAVE NEVER SEEN A TAX WE DIDN'T LIKE."

Mrs. Us could see that Sonny was rather upset with conditions. She was glad to hear him order some of the employees, who were milling about, to throw out all of the bad flux, sweep the floor, and clean up the room. Then he turned to Mrs. Us, pointed to his bag marked *The Right Flux*, and said, "This flux will work in your melting pot."

"What is this flux, and what do you call it?" Mrs. Us asked.

"I'm almost afraid to tell you the main ingredient," Sonny replied. "You know the new words they are using these days. I hear that some committee is working on new definitions of *left* and *right*. I believe the preferred new terms are *left* is *right* and *right* is *wrong*, or is it *wrong* is *right?*

"Before I say the word for the major ingredient of this flux, let me read you something that happened almost 2,000 years ago when the Chief Designer was in Jerusalem on special assignment." With this, Sonny reached in his briefcase and taking out a well-worn Book said, "This was our Textbook in the school of melting-pot engineering. It provides definitions and values of standards that haven't changed for centuries. It's sort of like your international MKS (meter, kilogram, second) standards. No good engineer would try working without proven standards these days." Sonny then continued, "A lawyer came to the Chief Designer and asked him 'Master what is the great commandment in the law?'" Then opening his book, Sonny started to read: "'*Jesus said unto him, Thou shalt love the Lord thy God with all thy heart, and with all thy soul, and with all thy mind. This is the first and great commandment. And the second is like unto it, Thou shalt love thy neighbor as thy self. On these hang all the law and the prophets.*'"[1]

"I know the word!" Mrs. Us injected. "It is LOVE. But who can love like that?"

Sonny waited a moment, and then said, "It isn't easy. In fact, without the Gift kit Nurse Trustworthy told you about while you were in the hospital, it is practically impossible." Then he flipped over a few pages and began to read again: *"I have declared unto them thy name, and will declare it: that the love wherewith Thou hast loved me may be in them, and I in them."*[2] "You see," he said, "with the new heart, God's love in you, and all the rest that you get with your Gift kit, it really can be done. With this kind of love, people of all races and colors can work together, and care for each other instead of fighting."

"What are the other ingredients?" Mrs. Us asked.

After a pause, Sonny replied, "The correct flux combination varies from time to time depending on conditions in the melting pot. Basically there are three main ingredients in melting-pot flux, but first let me tell you something that happened about 2,600 years ago. There was a melting pot that had been doing quite well, and then got into real trouble. Dr. Wisdom sent a heavyset gentleman with a sad face, to warn them that it needed fixing. Seems that things were very similar to your problem." With this, Sonny took out his Textbook and started to read:

And they will deceive every one his neighbor, and will not speak the truth: they have taught their tongue to speak lies, and weary themselves to commit iniquity .... For death is come up into our windows, and is entered into our palaces, to cut off our children from without, and the young men from the streets."[3]

Sonny paused for breath and said, "Almost sounds like your evening news Mrs. Us! Now let me read more of what God told the prophet. *'Thus saith the Lord, Let not the wise man glory in his wisdom, neither let the mighty man glory in his might, let not the rich man glory in his riches: But let him that glorieth glory in this, that he understandeth and knoweth me, that I am the Lord which exercise **loving kindness, judgment, and righteousness** in the earth: for in these I delight, saith the Lord.'"*[4] Looking up at Mrs. Us he said, "You see, here are the three most important ingredients in melting-pot flux. They are: love, judgment, and righteousness—justice if you prefer. The percentages required depend on conditions in the pot. Some times an 80-10-10 mix will do fine when things are functioning properly. This happens when children are raised with clear boundaries of right and wrong, when they are made to realize that they are responsible for their actions, and when they are taught to provide for their own needs and to help those about them.

"Now, Mrs. Us, you have a problem, as you saw, from your charts in the hospital. This happened when the activists who had more energy than knowledge started to throw in their new flux combinations. To fix things up, I have added some big doses of judgment and righteousness to the first few batches of *The Right Flux*. It is up to you to add this flux. I heard some talk at headquarters that if you don't start adding the right flux soon, the Almighty may add some flux of his own—*with a high judgment content!*

"You also have a problem with all those in your melting pot who have no knowledge or fear of God. Many of them have become hardened criminals. Others sitting in plush offices are stealing billions from the taxpayers. These can only be fixed by getting new hearts from their Gift kits. To help them make the right choice, I overheard that Headquarters will be sending Dr. Bible Truth, and many others like him who also preach and practice God's Word, to speak to you. They will urge you to have all in your melting pot pick up their Gift boxes while there is still time. They will also urge all who have picked up their Gift boxes to read and follow their Instruction Book."

Sonny took a poster from his briefcase. He handed it to Mrs. Us and said, "Here are the instructions to post in your melting pot room. Now I must hurry to my next assignment. There are lots of places having trouble with their melting pots." Then he gave Mrs. Us a hug and said, "I hope you are feeling better next time I stop by," and then hurried back to his boat.

INSTRUCTIONS FOR OPERATION OF MELTING POTS
  1. Control the temperature carefully:
     a. Treat all with equal justice.,
     b. Provide a safe environment for all.
     c. See that judgment is executed fairly and quickly.

2. Watch the stirring rate:
   a. Think out changes carefully.
   b. Don't vacillate or keep changing the rules.
   c. Beware of complacency.
   d. Beware of small pressure groups seeking their own self-interests.
3. Add the right flux regularly:
   a. Beware of super-charismatic persons gathering followers to themselves instead of turning men's hearts to God.
   b. Look for leaders with *integrity* and *stability*, those promoting good goals for the country.
   c. Encourage everyone in the melting pot to read their Instruction Book each day.
4. The right flux. *"Love is patient; love is kind and envies no one. Love is never boastful, nor conceited, nor rude; never selfish, nor quick to take offense. Love keeps no score of wrongs; does not gloat over other men's sins, but delights in the truth."*[5] Add justice, judgment, love, and enough compassion and forgiveness to fill the cup.

CHAPTER NOTES

My friend, you and I are in Mrs. Us's melting pot. Are we adding the right flux—the giving LOVE of God—to this melting pot we live in? Mrs. Us doesn't need more of the sensual self-seeking emotions mistakenly called love. She needs true healing LOVE—the kind of love that caused Mother Teresa to give of herself to help the poor and needy. The kind of love that causes a caring teacher to put in long hours helping to shape the lives of the children entrusted to her. The kind of love that causes a parent to discipline a child. The kind of love that makes a public official give up a chance for monetary gain to stand for what is right; or that causes you to call a friend just to let him know that you care. This love may be as simple as a friendly smile that comes from a heart at peace with God. When this type of flux is added, Mrs. Us's melting pot will once again be a safe and enjoyable place to live.

---

[1] Matthew 22: 37-39, KJV

[2] John 17:26, KJV

[3] Jeremiah 9:5, 21, KJV

[4] Jeremiah 9: 23-24, KJV

[5] 1 Corinthians 13:4-6, NEB

CHAPTER 3

MOTHER EARTH VISITS MRS. US

WHY DO NATIONS DIE?

THERE WAS A LOUD KNOCK AT HER DOOR, AND MRS. US HURRIED DOWN THE STAIRS. ON OPENING HER FRONT DOOR, SHE SAW A RATHER ROUND LADY WITH WHAT SEEMED LIKE A CLOUD FOR her hat. She seemed remarkably well-preserved for her age. In fact Mrs. Us was not sure if this was an older-looking young person or a young-looking old person. Her visitor smiled, held out her hand, and said, "Good morning, Mrs. Us. They call me Mother Earth."

The strength of her handshake surprised Mrs. Us, who by now was convinced that Mother Earth was quite a bit her elder. Then she replied, "Please come in. It's very nice to see you."

As they climbed the stairs, Mrs. Us had to stop for breath and was surprised that her visitor didn't seem to mind the climb. When they reached the living room, Mother Earth exclaimed, "My dear, you really have a beautiful view of the harbor."

"Yes, I am always glad to get back home," Mrs. Us replied. "Those trips to Washington have been rather trying lately."

"I know what you mean," her visitor replied. "In fact, I came to see you about your doctors in Washington. Many of them are confused and all upset over my health, when you are the one who really needs help."

"I believe," Mrs. Us said, "that one of them, Dr. Partly Cloudy, wrote that you were having trouble with all the CO_2 in the air and that you were about to suffer heat prostration. I must admit, though, that you look remarkably cool to me right now."

"Yes," Mother Earth replied, "He and other environmental writers have convinced many of your school children and even some of your doctors on the Hill that CO_2 is really bad stuff. You know that back in the beginning, when the Almighty created me, CO_2 in my atmosphere was, and still is, the key to life on my globe. Without it, physical life as you know it could not exist. It is true that we should be careful about our environment, but the pollution that should really be worrying you the most now is not CO_2 or ozone, but two preventable environmental scourges. I don't have time now, but I'll come back tomorrow morning and tell you what they are and more about CO_2. Now I must tell you of two times in the past when man's actions really changed my environment.

"But before I do I should remind you that I'm really nobody's mother. I just provide a living space for all the creatures placed here by the Creator. You know, things were different back on day six when God said, 'Let Us make man in Our image, after Our likeness: and let them have dominion over the fish of the sea, and over the fowl of the air, and over the cattle, and over all the earth….' Adam and Eve enjoyed living in my garden. I was young and beautiful. There were no thorns or thistles, no death, and my climate was just right. Of all the creatures placed on me, man was unique. He was given the **right of dominion** and the **right of choice**.

"One day Arch Enemy deceived Eve into believing that God didn't really mean what He had said about not eating the fruit from the tree of the knowledge of good and evil. Eve saw that the fruit looked good and after she had eaten, gave it to Adam, who joined her in making the choice to disobey the Creator's only **do not** command. I well remember that day and the results of man making the wrong choice. They suffered spiritual death and started to die physically. Because Adam disobeyed the Creator, God cursed me, and my environment really changed for the worse. Arch Enemy grabbed the right of dominion, thorns, thistles, and weeds of all kinds started to grow, and things started to die."

Mother Earth paused for breath and produced Chart 1 which she handed to Mrs Us. "As you can see from this chart, most of these early men had life spans of more than nine hundred years. This went on for 10 generations—over 1600 years. The one exception you see in genera-

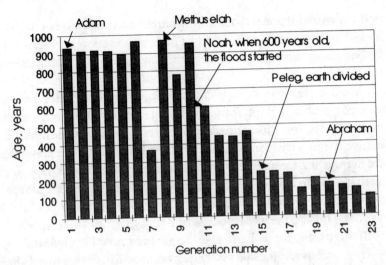

CHART 1. MAN'S CHANGING LIFE SPANS FROM ADAM TO JOSEPH

tion seven was Enoch. God enjoyed walking with Enoch so much that one day when he was 365 years old they just walked right up to heaven.

"By the time Noah was born in 1056 AA (after Adam) things really got bad. '*The earth was corrupt before God, and the earth was filled with violence.*'[1] That sounds like some of your cities today, Mrs. Us! Then the Almighty decided to wipe out the whole violent and disease-ridden population in a world-wide flood. But since Noah pleased God, He instructed him to build an ark. The year that Noah turned 600, the ark was finished, Methuselah died, and the flood came. Only Noah and his family who were in the ark remained alive."

Mother Earth paused for breath, and Mrs. Us saw a tear in her eye as she continued in a sad voice. "This time, man's actions really changed my environment drastically, I almost got wiped out in the flood! My climate changed dramatically, and man's lifespan dropped to about 450 years. Noah, however, lived out his full 950 years. Then some time about 1800 years AA, in Peleg's days when the earth was divided, things got worse, and as you see, man's life span took another big decrease. In another ten to fifteen generations the life span dropped to about its present level."

Mrs. Us, who had been listening intently to the account of early man

43

and his changing longevity, said, "Mother Earth, why do nations die, and what is the life span for someone like me? You know that during my last visit to the hospital in Washington, I wondered if my condition was terminal."

"You are 217 years old now," Mother Earth replied. "That's near the average age of nations on my globe. Like people, some nations seem to die in infancy, some like Yugoslavia die at an early age, while others far outlive the average. For example, England is over 600. You know that the average life span of your citizens increased from about 40 at your birth in 1776 to almost 80 now. In spite of this, the maximum life span did not change, and is still around 100 to 120 like it was when Joseph was in Egypt 1700 years before Christ."

At this point, Mother Earth said, "I must leave now. I saw Nurse Trustworthy in town and she said that she was coming to see you today. When she stops by, you can ask her about the life spans of men and nations. Thanks for the visit. I'll see you tomorrow morning," she called out as she was leaving.

Her visitor had hardly gone when Mrs. Us looked out her window and saw a boat pulling up to her dock. When she saw Nurse Trustworthy get off the boat, she hurried down the stairs as fast as she dared. When she reached the door, Nurse Trustworthy, who was waiting for her, embraced Mrs. Us and exclaimed, "And how is my favorite patient!" They walked slowly up the stairs while discussing things that had happened since their last meeting in the hospital. Once upstairs, the nurse handed Mrs. Us a bag with some fresh bagels she had just bought on Long Island. Mrs. Us put on a pot of coffee, and they sat down to enjoy a mid-morning snack.

Soon, Mrs. Us was telling her nurse about her earlier visitor. She showed her the chart of life spans that Mother Earth had left and said, "This paints a different picture than I have seen in some of my museums and books. Many of them show man starting from some simple life form and after millions of years evolving into a monkey and eventually into modern man. From what Mother Earth has told me, it sounds like man has been descending rather than ascending as the books on evolution claim. I also have been wondering, why do nations die, and how long do I have to live?"

Her nurse replied, "First let me tell you about people, and then we will talk about nations. You know there is soft science that involves theory and imagination. There is also hard science that is based on observed facts. Evolution starts with a theory, and tries to find observations to support it. Since no one has seen evolution from one species to another occur, they are forced to look at fossils and bones and then, using a good deal of imagination and a fill-in-the-blanks approach, they arrive at a nice looking diorama. This is soft science.

"The Creation record in Genesis simply states what God told Moses. Hard science can be applied to evaluate the validity of both the creation record and the theory of evolution. One of the major problems with evolution theory is that the details keep changing as man attempts to reconcile differences with new scientific discoveries. The Genesis account, on the other hand, is fixed and is not in conflict with the facts of hard science.

"The Almighty designed and created Adam, a man who could have lived on forever, but when he chose to disobey God, death entered the scene. You might call this choice and consequences. In the past 40 years since the discovery of the DNA molecule in 1953 we have gained a greater insight into life, and yes, even death. Here was the amazing discovery that each cell in your body contains a blueprint unique to your body.

"Testing of cells grown *in vitro* showed that they could replicate, but eventually aged and died after a number of replications. In addition, they apparently could do minor repairs if damaged. This may result from what communication engineers call error-detecting and error-correcting codes. The upper limit of cell replications possible in animals and man seemed to vary from around 10 times for mice that live for about 3 years to about 50 to 60 times for man who has a maximum life span at present of around 120 years. In general, the number of possible cell replications appears to increase with the maximum age of the species.[2]

"Cell replacement in the human body is far more complex. There are blood cells, fat cells, muscle cells, bone cells, and many others, all different and yet all containing the same unique DNA blueprint. The replacement rate is different for the various cells. Skin cells, for example, are replaced often while others like nerve and brain cells at one time appeared to never be replaced.[3] Recent studies indicate that even these cells, when supplied with a hormone called nerve growth factor, may be able to be repaired or rejuvenated.[4] The actual maximum life span of the total body is governed by a number of factors. These include: inherited genes, environmental factors, the health of a person's immune system which eliminates defective and diseased cells, the availability of good food, and the right trace elements. There is also no doubt that the mind plays a very important role in the overall functioning, health, and life span of the body. *Prevention* magazine recently wrote that *all deaths before age 120 are premature.*

"The things which can damage cells include: ultraviolet light, high energy particles, oxidants, toxic chemicals, and of course, excess heat. It is interesting that oxygen, which is essential for life, can also destroy the cells or cause them to become cancerous. There is some evidence that strong magnetic fields may interfere with the cell reproduction process. In addition to the cell replacement process in the individual, there is the passing on of physical life to the next generation. We are well aware of the fact that when there is gene damage then genetic defects can be passed down to a person's offspring.

"Prior to the Genesis flood, the Bible tells us that there was a mantle of water above the atmosphere. This could have reduced the ultraviolet light at the earth's surface. Since there is no mention of rain or rainbows before the flood, it also appears that there was little if any atmospheric dust or radioactive material to be drawn into the lungs. These two factors would reduce cell damage far below present levels. As a result Adam could easily have passed on to the next nine generations the ability to live for over nine hundred years."

Mrs. Us, who had been taking this all in, injected, "What happened at the flood to change things?"

Nurse Trustworthy replied, "We are told that the fountains of the great deep were broken up, and the windows of heaven were opened. It sounds like a lot of volcanic activity as well as a collapse of the water canopy. This would increase the ultraviolet light, and since some volcanoes eject uranium, they could have introduced a lot of radioactive dust into the air. Noah's son Shem appeared to suffer some damage and only lived to be 600. His life-extending genes may have suffered damage, since the next three generations only lived to be about 440 years old. Starting with Peleg, in whose days the earth was divided, something else drastic appears to have happened since the life span of the next three generations drops to 230 years. From here on life spans decrease slowly down to Joseph (generation 23) who only lived to 110 years. This is a span attainable by some today where we are at about generation 130."

Mrs. Us exclaimed, "My, wouldn't a lot of my citizens like to live a healthy life up to 900! Just think of how much you could learn and do with that kind of a life span. I'm sure that my scientists who are studying DNA would like to have a chance to look at some of Noah's DNA." Mrs. Us, who was anxious to hear something about her *own* life expectancy, asked, "How long do you think I'll live?"

Her nurse replied, "The Almighty is the only One who knows the answer to that, but I'll see if Headquarters is willing to send someone to tell you what might happen. God has not set an upper limit on the life span of nations, but it is clear that He cuts off some nations when they turn from Him. The secret of God's dealings with nations was revealed to Daniel some 600 years before Christ when he wrote, '*Blessed be the name of God forever and ever; For wisdom and might are His: And He changeth the times and seasons; He removes kings, and raises up kings: He gives wisdom to the wise, and knowledge to those who have understanding.*'[5] Your founding fathers wrote that men were judged in the next life, but since there was no life after death for nations, they would be rewarded or judged *during their lifetime.* For example, Thomas Jefferson wrote, '*And can the liberties of a nation be thought secure when we have removed their only firm basis, a conviction in the minds of the people that these liberties are the gift of God? That they are not to be violated but with His wrath? Indeed I tremble for my country when I reflect that God is just; that His justice cannot sleep forever.*'[6]

"In a way, your Constitution is like the inherited DNA molecule of a person. You, Mrs. Us, received a good constitution, but as the founding fathers said, it was written for primarily moral, law-abiding citizens.

'We have no Government armed with power capable of contending with human passions unbridled by morality and religion…Our Constitution was made only for a moral and religious people. It is wholly inadequate to the government of any other.'[7] Your citizens are like cells in your body. If a lot of them become sick or cancerous, you can not stay in good health. Just as with man and other living organisms, there are factors which damage the life-extending capability of nations. Some of these are: war, natural environmental change, and economic problems. The primary reason for the fall of a nation is usually the moral decay of its citizens. Samuel Adams, known as the Father of the American Revolution, wrote in 1772, 'When the people are virtuous they can not be subdued; but once they lose their virtue they will be ready to surrender their liberties to the first external or internal invader…if virtue and knowledge are diffused among the people, they will never be enslaved. This will be their great security.'[8]

"One of the important parts of your Constitution is the claim of 'liberty and justice for all.' Liberty and freedom in a nation are like oxygen for the living body, which we saw to be essential—and yet dangerous in the form of some oxidants. You have seen how in the 1960s under the guise and banner of liberty, that many of your citizens lost a great deal of their freedom! Grown men, lawyers and judges who should have known better, took away the freedom of your children to pray or read the Bible in school. Loss of freedom is like cell damage. The effects may not be noticed until some time later. Mrs. Us, you saw the tragic results of this loss of freedom in the charts we showed you back in the Washington hospital. The greatest antioxidant for man, that prevents moral decay and damage to your cells (your citizens), is God's Word. Like most medicines and vitamins, it works best when taken daily.

"Now I must leave, but I'll call Headquarters to see if they can send someone from the Watcher's Office to tell you about your life expectancy. You know, the Watchers keep track of the status of nations and rulers. They even know more about you than your Office of Management and Budget." Nurse Trustworthy bent over and kissed Mrs. Us on the forehead. "Don't get up, my dear. Get some rest," she said, and hurried down the stairs.

Mrs. Us, who had been sitting on the sofa, decided to lay her head down and close her eyes. Thoughts of early man's changing life span, the effects of choice on environments, and of course her own life expectancy kept running through her mind. As she dozed off, a tall white-robed man with a kindly face seemed to appear out of nowhere.

In a soft but firm voice her visitor started to speak, "Mrs. Us, I have been sent to tell you about choices and your life expectancy. Your nurse told you about the four primary causes of death for a nation: 1) war, 2) weather and natural disasters, 3) economic failure, and 4) moral decay. Often all are involved, but almost always the last, moral decay, must be present. You see, a nation whose people have a firm moral basis can overcome the effects of the other three. We Watchers have seen many nations, rulers, and cities rise and fall. One of us told Nebuchadnezzar what would happen to him in the days of Daniel.[9] We watched the city of Port Royal, Jamaica, when it was the center for pirates that preyed on shipping between Europe and the Americas. It became known as Sodom because of its evil lifestyle. We saw it sink into the sea when the earthquake struck in June of 1692. The Almighty is still giving you the right of choice in this timeless message: '*Today I offer you the choice of life and good, or death and evil. If you obey the commands of the Lord your God which I give you this day, by loving the Lord your God, by conforming to His ways, and by keeping His commandments, statutes and laws, then you will live and increase, and the Lord your God will bless you ... But if your heart turns away and you do not listen ... you will not live long...*'[10] Your life expectancy, Mrs. Us, depends on the choices made by your people. Right now many of those being chosen for high offices in your government have hearts that have turned away from the Almighty and His ways. He is the one who will make the decision regarding your life span. I, as a Watcher, can only tell you, based on what I am seeing, that if you continue with your present trend, you will not have long to live. This can be changed if enough of your people return to conforming to the ways of God and keeping His commandments."

"You still have many enemies in the world and can not afford to allow you military strength to be weakened. The former USSR contries still have many nuclear weapons, and in addiition, you still have to face the growing possibility of ICBMs in the hands of terrorist nations. This requires a new approach to be prepared for such treats.

Then the Watcher disappeared as quickly as he had appeared, and Mrs. Us awoke with a start to find it was time for supper. After eating she went to bed early to be ready for Mother Earth's return in the morning.

CHAPTER NOTES

My friend, choices are still important in determining our environment. Often we do not realize the full impact of our choices, and the importance of making the right one. For example, in the early days of DDT, it was looked upon by those who used it as a wonderful choice. It was only later that its global harmful effects became evident. Similarly, the men who chose the design of the Chernobyl nuclear power plant, I am sure, thought they were making a good choice that would be helpful to many. Little did they know of the suffering and death that would result from that choice! When the Nine Specialists bowed to the pressures of a so-called civil liberties group in the 60s, few could foresee the great cost to the nation of that choice in loss of freedom, growing crime, and moral decay. Thanks to the concerted efforts of a few dedicated Christian lawyers, recent decisions of the Supreme Court have restored some of the freedoms lost. Unfortunately, there are still those who are actively working to take away the freedom God intended you to have.

The most important collective choice we can make is to return our nation to being "One Nation Under God." The real issue is to return to freedom under God: This is what made America great. To accomplish this we must:

1) Free our children to pray and read their Bible where and when they desire.

2) Free our companies from the crushing burden of big government with its endless and ever-changing regulations, and excessive tax burdens.

3) Free ourselves from the dangerous dependence on foreign energy sources.

4) Free ourselves from the huge debt hanging over our head, and not try to solve all problems by more spending.

The road back to freedom will be difficult. It will take time and much wisdom to wean us from dependency on big government. The recent way that people in the great flood of '93 pulled together, and the way help was sent from all over the nation show that LOVE and human kindness are not dead in our land. We will make it if we turn to God for His help, and see that big government takes the essential, but not easy, step of downsizing and returns to governing with a light but fair and just hand.

If you, my reader, are one who has accepted the great Gift of God, join me in praying for our country. If you have not yet taken this most important step, I urge you to accept the *Gift* that will give you true personal freedom and peace with your Creator.

---

[1] Genesis 6:11, KJV

[2] Kahn, Carol; *Beyond the Helix DNA and the quest for longevity*, Times Books, 1985

[3] Brand, Paul and Yancey, Philip; *Fearfully and Wonderfully Made*, Zondervan Publishing House, 1980

[4] "Aging on Hold," *Chicago Tribune*, Dec. 13, 1991

[5] Daniel 2:20-21, NKJV

[6] Thomas Jefferson, *Writings of Thomas Jefferson*, Albert Bergh, editor, Thomas Jefferson Memorial Assoc., 1904, Vol. II, p. 227.

[7] John Adams, *The Works of John Adams*, Vol IX, p. 229.

[8] McDowell and Beliles, *America's Providential History*, p. 93

[9] See for example, Daniel 4:13

[10] Deuteronomy 30:15-17, NEB

[11] 1 Corinthians 6:9-10, NKJV

[12] Leviticus 18:22-25, NASB

CHAPTER 4

MRS. US AND THE ENVIRONMENT

THE REAL POLLUTION PROBLEMS

THE NEXT MORNING, MOTHER EARTH RETURNED RIGHT ON TIME AS PROMISED. UNDER HER ARM WAS A NEWSPAPER WITH THE HEADLINE, "SAVE THE EARTH FROM CO_2 AND GLOBAL WARMING." When they sat down, Mother Earth exclaimed, "They all seem to think carbon dioxide (CO_2) is a major pollution problem these days! As I told you yesterday, you have two far more serious environmental pollution problems. They are violent *crime* and promiscuous and perverted *sex*. Believe me, these problems are reducing the quality of your environment far more than atmospheric carbon dioxide! The sad thing is they could easily have been prevented. Remember how early man's actions changed my environment in the past. Now the actions of your people are causing serious social and economic environmental problems. Violent crime has made it unsafe for many of your people to walk the streets of your cities, and sex out of control has increased disease and suffering throughout your land. In addition, the Creator has warned you that both of these practices can bring about other serious natural environmental consequences.

"Since the flood in Noah's days, there have been ups and downs in my temperature and climate. Living conditions have been very severe at times, and in spite of the two major man-induced global environmental changes I described to you yesterday, I still try to provide a beautiful, bountiful place for all. Some are trying to keep it that way while they enjoy the bounty I provide. Others think I'm a frail old lady with one foot in the grave and the other on a banana peel. Then there are some, like Mr. Sadman, who try to make me a sad place to live. He recently polluted my soil with the blood of innocent men, my air with the smoke from hundreds of burning oil wells, and my water with oil."

At this point, Mother Earth looked at her watch and exclaimed, "I really must be rolling along. It wouldn't do for me to get everyone else's clock out of step," she said with a twinkle in her eye. "This morning I saw your friend Sonny along with Dr. Truth in town. They both said that they were planning to visit you soon. When Sonny stops by, ask him about CO_2 and my temperature control system. He can tell you some of the details. Yes, and ask Dr. Truth about the two preventable environmental scourges. Thanks for the visit," she called out. Then seeming almost to roll down the stairs, she was gone.

This whirlwind visit from Mother Earth was almost too much for Mrs. Us, so she laid her head down on the sofa and fell fast asleep. Soon she started to dream that she was back in the Washington hospital operating room with a team of doctors leaning over her. They seemed to be talking about ways to get more money out of the patient. She heard one say, "We can really increase our fee this time if we can convince her that an energy tax is essential to getting her CO_2 level down."

One of the other doctors said, "Maybe we could tax at the business level, and she wouldn't know we were doing it."

Mrs. Us awoke with a start, "I hope that was only a dream!" she exclaimed. "I do hope that Sonny stops by soon so I can ask him about CO_2 and Mother Earth."

After supper, Mrs. Us found she couldn't get her mind off her energy needs. She kept thinking that energy was essential to the existence of all her people. How, she wondered, can an energy tax help my industries compete on a global market? Realizing that she was getting nowhere, she decided to climb into bed.

ATMOSPHERIC CARBON DIOXIDE AND CLIMATE CHANGE

Early the next morning her phone rang. It was Sonny calling to say he would like to stop by to see her. Mrs. Us was delighted, and told him to come right over. Soon Sonny's boat arrived, and when Mrs. Us greeted him she asked, "Sonny, how are the other melting pots doing?"

"Some good news, but still lots of bad news," he replied. "There was some improvement in Somalia, but there is still much to be done. They really haven't started working on the root cause of the problem, you know, the need to add the right flux. I also stopped in some other African countries. What a shame to see the large numbers dying from AIDS brought on by sodomy and sexual promiscuity. This could have been prevented if they had only read and heeded the Instruction Book that was made available to them. Some of these African, as well as other melting pots, are in serious trouble. Arch Enemy seems to have his helpers working overtime stirring up trouble."

Looking for a more cheery subject, Mrs. Us said, "Sonny, can you come upstairs and tell me something about atmospheric CO_2?"

"Sounds like you've been talking to Mother Earth," he replied. "Lots of activists have gotten all heated up over this subject lately." Arriving upstairs, Mrs. Us poured some tea and Sonny started to talk. "Many have come to think of CO_2 as an atmospheric pollutant. Actually, it's one of the essential keys to all life on this planet. Carbon dioxide is the basic raw material that plants use in photosynthesis to convert solar energy into food, fiber, and wood. Today the average CO_2 level in the atmosphere is about 360 parts per million (ppm). Most plants grow faster and bigger with an increase in CO_2 levels. The way they respond depends on the type of pathway used in the photosynthetic fixation of carbon dioxide.[1] C3 plants, which start with 3 carbon atoms per molecule, show the greatest response to increased levels of carbon dioxide. Most green plants, including trees, algae, and most food crops, use the C3 pathway. A doubling of carbon dioxide levels shows yield increases of from 25 to 64 percent for cereal grains."

Mrs. Us, who had been listening carefully, said, "It looks like *plants* really like carbon dioxide, Sonny, but how about the *weather*?"

"I'll get to that soon," Sonny said, "but first look at Chart 1, which shows estimated global exchanges of CO_2 with the atmosphere.[2] The upward-pointing arrows are injection rates of carbon dioxide into the atmosphere expressed in metric tons of carbon dioxide per year. You can see that man's input is about one tenth that from natural sources. The downward pointing arrows represent removal rates in the same

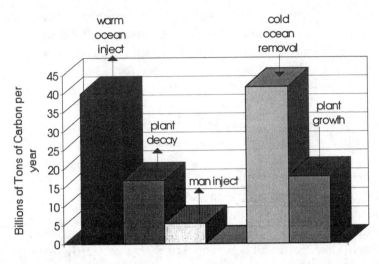

CHART 1. ANNUAL ADDITIONS OF CO_2 TO THE ATMOSPHERE.

units. Trees and tundra are important *scrubbers* (means of removing carbon dioxide from the atmosphere). The oceans, however, appear to be the largest factor in the global exchange cycle. Their role in removing carbon dioxide in the cold oceans and injecting it into the atmosphere from the warm oceans is very complex. Some of the important factors are temperature, pH, surface roughness, photosynthesis, nutrients, coral reef growth, and ocean currents, including local up-welling."

"Sounds complicated," Mrs. Us said. "It looks like we should be very careful with our oceans. But isn't it true that both CO_2 levels and global temperatures are increasing?"

Sonny replied, "Yes, CO_2 levels have been increasing for the past 200 years as shown in Chart 2. It can also be seen that temperatures have both increased and decreased over the interval shown. The temperatures shown are the annual average values for Basel, Switzerland, which has kept one of the longest records available. If one takes the interval from 1890 to 1950, it looks like temperatures go up with increasing CO_2 values. On the other hand, the intervals from 1860 to 1890 or from

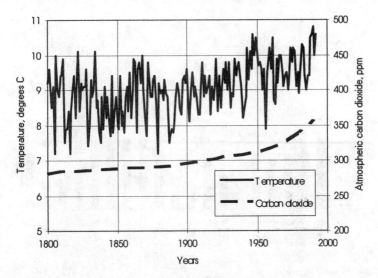

CHART 2. TEMPERATURES AT BASEL SWITZERLAND, AND ATMOSPHERIC CO_2 LEVELS.

1950 to 1970 show temperatures decreasing while CO_2 levels continue to increase. Similar variations are found when examining average northern hemisphere temperatures. There are many factors, including solar radiation, involved in regulating the earth's temperature. Several of the important ones on earth are: clouds, water vapor, CO_2 levels, and atmospheric dust loading.

"It's important to note that doubling CO_2 concentration in the atmosphere does not mean that the so-called green house effect doubles. This is because the CO_2 molecules are wavelength-selective in their absorption. Sort of like a color filter that attenuates a narrow band of color and lets all the rest of the light pass through. Once you are taking most of a given narrow color band out it doesn't make much difference in the overall light transmitted if you take all of that color out. Another important thing to remember is that when CO_2 levels rise, plants in general grow faster. This tends to scrub carbon dioxide out of the atmosphere at a faster rate. The earth is dynamic, and all of the factors shown in Chart 1 change with time. Chart 3 shows the estimated annual human injections of CO_2 into the atmosphere expressed in parts per mil-

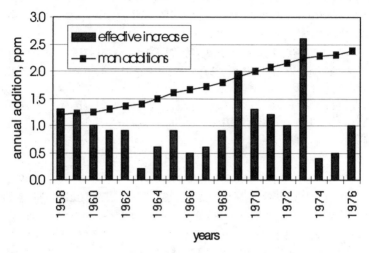

CHART 3. ANNUAL ADDITIONS OF CO_2 INTO THE ATMOSPHERE.

lion of the total atmospheric mass.[3] Also shown are the effective increases in CO_2 loading for each year based on observations at Hawaii.[4] The average effective additions over the time interval shown are about 0.4 times the man-injected values. It is clear from the large amount of variability that the natural input and scrubbing rates are dominant.

"The atmospheric dust loading, high in the stratosphere, produces global cooling as the dust acts like a shade that reduces the amount of solar energy reaching the earth's surface. The primary source of stratospheric dust is from volcanic activity, although there is some cosmic dust input. In 1883 the eruption of Krakatoa, in Indonesia, injected an estimated 50 million metric tons of dust into the stratosphere. This was followed by the year without a summer. A similar and even larger event occurred in 1816 following the 1815 eruption of Tomboro, also in Indonesia. Crops were destroyed in New England which experienced frost and snow for most of the year. One Vermont farmer was frozen to death when he lost his way going to his barn during the great snowstorm of June 17, 1816.[5]

"Records show that volcanic activity occurs in cycles. These cycles appear to be related to crustal tidal forces that are influenced by the location of the sun, the earth, and the moon. There is considerable evidence that at one time the earth's cold regions were quite warm. For example, coal deposits are found in Antarctica, and large numbers of mammoths, saber-toothed tigers and other animals have been found buried in Siberia and Alaska. While examining ice cores from Greenland and Antarctica, researchers using oxygen 18 differences have found evidences that these cold regions were once quite warm.

"The earth's temperature-regulating system involves a number of beautifully interrelated mechanisms that are still not completely understood. It is also important not to rule out solar variations, as suggested in recent findings by the Danish Meteorological Institute. During the last solar cycle the total solar irradiance was remarkably stable with variations of about 0.1%. Examination of stars similar to our sun have shown that much larger variations are possible. Studies have indicated that even a 1% variation in solar brightness would have an effect equal to all the greenhouse gasses expected to accumulate during the next 40 years.[6] For a number of centuries prior to A. D. 1400, the northern hemisphere was quite warm. In the 1400s there was a large cooling followed by some warming in the 1500s, but in the 1600s there was a very cold spell often referred to as 'the little ice age of the 17th century.'

"The earth is very resilient, as observed in the rapid recovery after the recent eruption of Mt. St. Helens. It is prudent to be careful of our natural environment, but it is also essential that we be careful of our social and economic environments. Actually, Mrs. Us, based on past records[7], you may be in more danger from a severe cooling event than from overheating. Some years have both record cold and record heat. It is always important to remember that human knowledge is still quite limited, and that it is the Chief Designer who holds the whole world in His hands."

Sonny's cellular phone rang, and when he finished talking, he said, "I have to make an urgent visit to a melting pot that is in trouble. Hope this information on carbon dioxide and climate variations has been helpful." With this he gave Mrs. Us a hug and ran off to his boat.

DR. TRUTH AND THE POLUTION OF VIOLENCE

Mrs. Us saw another boat approaching and waited to see who her next visitor would be. When he set foot on her dock, she recognized him as Dr. Truth. On his arrival at the door, he took her hand in both of his and said, "Mrs. Us, it is good to see that you are up and about." When they reached her sitting room, Dr. Truth, as always, got right to the point. "I've come to warn you about two epidemics that will have a really serious effect on your health unless you take some corrective measures right away. The first is that you have too much violence and killing. Nurse Trustworthy showed you some of this on your charts back in the hospital. Violent killings are widespread. Children are randomly shooting children in your city streets. It is beginning to sound like the times that Moses wrote about before the flood. *'The earth was corrupt before God, and the earth was filled with violence.*'[8]

"Many are preaching tolerance these days. Tolerance of the wrong things can be very bad. You, Mrs. Us, have grown tolerant to violence and killing. We seem to blame society instead of the criminals committing the crimes. God spoke of the land being polluted with innocent blood. This is your land, and your problem. Your children are far more likely to suffer from robbery, rape, murder, and death from AIDS than from the problems of an overheated Mother Earth. This scourge of violence can be removed, but it will not be easy. It requires a change in people's hearts.

"You must reinstate values and virtue. Criminal behavior must not be tolerated. These steps are necessary but not enough. Some like to blame poverty for crime, but poverty was not the cause of your recent Los Angeles riots.[9] Greed, selfishness, and hatred were just waiting for an excuse to satisfy themselves. This can only be countered by LOVE— the true love of God. This type of love was demonstrated during the recent LA riots. Ex-convict Bennie Newton, a black man whose heart had been changed by God, came to the rescue of Fidel Lopez. Rioters had punched and kicked Lopez almost to death, torn off his clothes, and spray painted his body black. Newton, with a Bible in his hand, ran up and threw himself over this stranger's body, yelling, "Kill him and you have to kill me, too." Dr. Truth went on to describe more of the gruesome details of this and other events during the riot.

Tears came to Mrs. Us's eyes as she thought of all the suffering of her children. "Something must be done," she said through her tears. "Something really must be done to stop this."

THE SCOURGE OF SEX OUT OF CONTROL

"Now," Dr. Truth said, "I must tell you of another serious scourge that is threatening your life. It is perverted and promiscuous sex out of control. This has led to an alarming increase in sexually-transmitted disease that could easily have been prevented. AIDS and other associated diseases are now costing you billions of dollars and driving up health care costs. If some realistic steps are not taken soon, you may not survive. Sonny has already told you about the sad conditions in Africa resulting from AIDS. For years, they have been practicing the *new liberal morality* now championed by many of your activists.

Sex and nuclear energy have a lot in common. When properly controlled, and in the right place, they each can be beneficial. When out of control, they both spell disaster. God's Instruction Book spells out details for sexual behavior which, if practiced, would have prevented the AIDS outbreak. Even now these simple no-cost rules would stop its spread and eventually allow it to die out.

"At present your government is distributing faulty information on *safe sex with condoms* which is not really safe and is not controlling the spread of AIDS. A similar situation occurred during the early atom bomb tests. At that time, many in your military were not warned of the true dangers of radiation. Some of them were sent to observe the blast and later to walk through highly radioactive zones. As a result of not being adequately warned, many men in the military suffered and died of radiation sickness. Today, many are sick and many more will die of AIDS because of inadequate warning, and the failure to heed the simple commands in God's Instruction Book. These two environmental scourges have a common cause. When writing to the Romans who were suffering from problems like yours, Paul wrote, '*because, although they knew God, they did not glorify Him as God, nor were thankful .... Therefore God also gave them up to uncleanness in the lusts of their hearts, to dishonor their bodies .... men with men committing what is shameful, and receiving in themselves the penalty of their error.*[10]

"Mrs. Us, we are instructed to love our neighbors, and that includes those who are homosexual. True love, however, does not condone practices that God condemns, such as sodomy, which resulted in two of every three new AIDS cases reported in 1987.[11] Homosexuals are reported to have a rate of alcoholism three times the national average.[12] These practices have resulted in death rates from suicide as well as death rates in auto accidents which are much above the national average. These practices also spread other contagious and infectious disease. True love will seek to help those who are trapped in drugs and sexual perversion to turn from a "*gay*" (but for many a sad and frustrating) lifestyle to a truly happy and joy-filled life. The trouble starts when men know *about* God, but don't glorify or obey Him as God, and are not thankful! When a person turns to God and makes the choice to accept His Gift of a new heart, God will help him to overcome the strong addictive forces of drugs, or of a homosexual life style."

Dr. Truth got up to leave. He placed his hand on Mrs. Us's shoulder, and in a kind but stern voice said, "Be sure to take the medicine I prescribed for you earlier, and don't put off taking the right steps to stop the spread of these two scourges. Don't bother coming downstairs, I can let myself out." Then he hurried down the stairs and was gone.

CHAPTER NOTES

Many are becoming frustrated with the actions of some of Mrs. Us's doctors in Washington. Some are encouraging practices condemned by God in the Bible. Some are proposing programs of taxation and controls that are leading the nation into bankruptcy. We must be careful of our natural environment, but we must also care for our social and economic environments. This should include expanded research into new low-polluting energy sources and new technologies which will strengthen our economic environment. We must not let the fear of global warming blind us to our far more serious social and economic environmental problems. There are still many potential enemies in this world. We should tell our representatives on the Hill to take actions which prevent destroying the morale and effectiveness of our military. An effective military depends on truth and trust within its ranks, not deception.

Unless we make some changes soon, it is possible that God will allow Mrs. Us to fall on more hard times so that those of us who know Him will be shaken out of our complacency, so that we will be forced to cry out to God for help. He may use hard times to show us the importance of teaching our children truths found in the Bible, and to inspire them to grow up to be loving and productive citizens. We must also realize the importance of helping everyone find useful and rewarding work. This requires that businesses be provided with a stable and fair environment free of excessive taxes and regulations.

If perhaps you are one who hasn't yet accepted your free Gift of eternal life that the Chief Designer is offering you, I urge you to accept this most valuable of all gifts. You are a unique person; there is no other you! No matter what you may have done in the past, God wants you to accept His Gift so that you can start living a challenging and satisfying life, so that He can spend time with you. This relationship will bring lasting peace and joy. Jesus is saying, "*Come to me, all you who labor and are heavy laden, and I will give you rest.*"[13] Our world is full of change, turmoil, and unrest. One of the greatest things in life is to have an unchanging friend that cares, that always loves you and will give you true peace and rest.

[1] Wittwer, Sylvan H. (professor emeritus of horticulture at Michigan State University), "FLOWER POWER," *Policy Review*, fall 1992, pp. 4 - 9

[2] Watt, Arthur D., "Placing Atmospheric CO_2 in Perspective," *IEEE Spectrum*, Nov. 1971

[3] Rotty, Ralph M., "Present and Future Production of CO_2, from Fossil Fuels—A Global Appraisal," *US DOE Report 001 Carbon Dioxide Effects Research and Assessment Program*, May, 1979.

[4] Bacastow, Robert B and Keeling, Charles D., "Models to Predict Future Atmospheric CO_2 Concentrations," *Ibid.*, pp. 72-90.

[5] *The Old Farmer's Almanac*, 1966, p 46.

[6] John Maulbetsch, "Solar Influences on Global Climate," *EPRI Research Letter*, June 1993.

[7] O. Pettersson, "Climatic variations in historic and prehistoric time," *Ur Svenska Hydrografisk-Biologiska Komissionens Skrifter, Haft. V.*, Oct. 1916.

[8] Genesis 6:11, KJV

[9] Whitman, David, *US. News and World Report*, May 31, 1993

[10] Romans 1: 21-27, NKJV

[11] *U S News and World Report*, Jan. 12, 1987

[12] *Wall Street Journal*, March 15, 1986

[13] Matthew 11:28, NKJV

CHAPTER 5

MRS. US: IN SEARCH OF HEALTH

MAKING THE RIGHT CHOICE

MRS. US HAD TURNED ON THE EVENING NEWS, AND NOW SHE WATCHED INTENTLY AS HER PRESIDENT DELIVERED HIS IMPASSIONED SPEECH ON HEALTH CARE REFORM. HER MIND drifted off for a moment as she thought of what a nice-looking young man she had for a president, and yes, there was the attractive and intelligent First Lady in the front row. Mrs. Us knew that this meeting must be very important, for here in the halls of Congress were assembled many influential men and women—those who had the appearance of holding the reigns of power in the world. But did they really, she wondered? She listened carefully because she still felt ill and she wondered if the new prescriptions being prepared by her president and his friends would provide the needed cure to bring her back to health.

After the speech she put her head down on her sofa and closed her eyes. Surely, she thought, to have the best of health care available to every one of my citizens is very desirable. But three questions kept coming up in her mind. 1) Why are so many of my people sick and requiring so much medical care? 2) Why does this present health care system cost so much? and 3) What will this proposed plan do to *my* health?

She couldn't help but think that first priority should be given to keeping her citizens in good health so that fewer would need to take high-priced drugs and to spend so much time in hospitals. She also wondered how can a new system administered and mandated by big government with big overhead really cost less? Her mind even flashed back to the question, Am I terminal? She further wondered, Will this new health care plan help me or make me worse? Finding no immediate answers, she dropped off into a fitful sleep.

THE WATCHER AND CAUSES OF ILL HEALTH

Suddenly she saw in her sleep a tall white-robed man she recognized as the Watcher she had seen following Mother Earth's visit.

"Mrs. Us," he said in a stern voice, "I have come with an answer to your first question, 'Why are so many of my people sick and requiring so much medical care?'" Then he said, "Come with me." Suddenly they were in a doctor's office where a well-dressed, middle-aged man was explaining to the doctor the pains in his chest that had started soon after losing his job a month earlier. The scene shifted and they were in a small room where a young mother was huddled in a corner with the shades drawn. There were the sounds of gang violence outside as the distraught mother tried to comfort her three children. Then the scene changed to the emergency room of a large hospital. A young boy with a bullet wound in his chest was struggling to stay alive. Across from him was a young woman who had taken an overdose of drugs, and next to her was a young man who appeared to be dying of AIDS.

Almost as quickly as they had gone, Mrs. Us found herself back home and the white-robed Watcher explained. "You see, Mrs. Us, the businessman and the young mother are typical of many of your people whose need for medical aid has been brought on by fear. The cause of the young boy's wound was violence, and the two young persons were suffering because of addictions to alcohol, tobacco, drugs, and promiscuous sex.

"Answers to most of these problems are found in God's Instruction Book which is collecting dust or even missing in many of your homes. This book tells how to overcome fear, and how parents are to instruct and discipline their children. Parents are told to teach God's commandments, and how prompt and fair punishment prevents children from becoming hardened criminals. It tells you to love your neighbor, not to kill him. It tells you how to avoid AIDS by not having casual or perverted sex, and even tells you about good food and the need for exercise." Mrs. Us wanted to ask the Watcher about her chances for recovery, but fearing he might give her an actual termination date, she decided to wait and talk to her friend Sonny.

The Watcher looked at Mrs. Us and said, "Remember, the major causes of ill health and the need of medical care are: **fear, violence, addictions, and ignorance.** Your medical, financial, and other serious problems will be greatly reduced if your people read and heed their Instruction Book." Then, as if he knew what Mrs. Us wanted to ask, he said "Your present ill health was brought on by spiritual decay, followed by moral decay, followed by financial decay. You are fast approaching the condition of those in Israel when the Almighty warned them, '*They are a nation that lacks good counsel, devoid of understanding. If only they had the wisdom to understand this and give thought to their end!*' [1] You, Mrs. Us, are in great need of 'good counsel.' You need men and women in Washington who can see the decay you are suffering and turn the nation back to 'One Nation under God.'" With this the Watcher vanished. Mrs. Us awoke and, seeing it was almost midnight, hurried off to bed.

OUR NURSE RETURNS

Early the next morning the phone rang, and a cheery voice said, "Good morning, Mrs. Us! I would like to stop by to see you." Mrs. Us was delighted to hear Nurse Trustworthy and suggested she come right over and join her for breakfast. After her nurse arrived, their conversation soon turned to health care, and Mrs. Us told her nurse about the Watcher's visit. Then she asked the nurse her second question, "Why does my medical care cost so much?"

Nurse Trustworthy replied, "Finance is not my specialty, but I have seen some of the bills being prepared and they are frightening. You know when the patient isn't paying directly, he has little incentive to question the high prices. For the large number of people on Medicare, once they have met their small minimum deductible there is no incentive to try and keep healthy or to care for their minor aches and pains when they can visit the doctor and hospital without any out-of-pocket expenses.

"I have also seen two other major problems that are responsible for the high cost of your health care. They both stem from one root-cause, a greedy litigation system. First, doctors have to order more tests for a patient than are actually needed to protect themselves from negligence suits, and second, doctors have to charge much more than is required to run their office and make a good living. This is because of frivolous and astronomically high liability suits. These have pushed insurance costs almost out of reach for many doctors. As a matter of fact, some doctors have actually closed their offices because of liability risks. Recently I heard that you, Mrs. Us, spend 650 percent more than the Japanese do in settling law suits.²"

Realizing that all this talk was not cheering her patient up, Nurse Trustworthy said, "This is a beautiful fall day. Let's go for a walk in the country and enjoy the autumn foliage."

As they walked along and saw the yellow, red, and golden leaves, Mrs. Us exclaimed, "What a great day to be alive and enjoy the Creator's handiwork!"

"Now, my dear, you are making progress," her nurse said, and thought to herself, "Maybe there is hope for a recovery." When they returned from their walk and lunch at a sidewalk cafe, they found a note on the door from Sonny. It said that he would return later in the afternoon. Nurse Trustworthy helped her patient up the stairs and suggested that she rest until Sonny arrived.

SONNY ON HEALTH AND THE ECONOMY

When Sonny arrived he was carrying his briefcase and had two newspapers under his arm. As he greeted her, Mrs. Us sensed that Sonny was not his usual cheery self. He showed her the headlines, U.S. SERVICEMEN KILLED IN SOMALIA, and RECORD NUMBER OF AMERICANS LIVING IN POVERTY. "Not very good news for you today," he said. "You did help stop starvation in Somalia, but their problem is that they have not been adding the right flux to their melting pot. All the UN and U.S. troops can't solve that problem. Trying to solve Somalia's problem by military force is costly to you in lives and money at a time when you can ill afford it. You have serious money and poverty problems of your own at home. Back in 1965 when President Johnson started his 'war on poverty,' you were spending under two billion dollars a year on health and Medicare costs. Now you are spending well over 200 billion a year on welfare, and are ending up with more persons on the poverty roles than when you started."

At this point, Mrs. Us told Sonny about her previous two visitors. Being anxious to get an answer to her last question, she asked, "What do you think the president's health plan will do for my health?"

Sonny replied, "Mrs. Us, your citizens presently have the best health care facilities in the world. However, it's true that they've become very expensive, and are not universally available to all. In many cases your system has become impersonal and lacks compassion. As you were told, much of the cost increases have resulted from growing legal costs as well as from violence, fear, AIDS, and addictions. The idea of free government health care to all sounds appealing, but it is important to note that governments do not provide health care, people do. Don't be misled! **People will pay,** not government or corporations.

"When a person develops good health habits and properly cares for his or her own body, this minimizes the health care needed from others. Your citizens should be encouraged to maintain good health and be rewarded for doing this.

"It's true that provision must be made for those in need. The Bible makes this abundantly clear. When Jesus walked this earth He healed the sick and showed compassion to those in need. His instructions to us are, '*A new commandment I give to you, that you love one another, even as I have loved you.*'[3] In your early days, most of the hospitals and shelters were run by and provided for by church groups. They were demonstrating God's type of love.

"Your government-run welfare system is often impersonal. It rewards many who could work, but don't want to work or save for future needs. It also penalizes those who are working and providing for their own needs. Freedom and self-reliance are important, and should not be traded for costly mandated insurance. Big government handouts often make 'dependent slaves' of welfare recipients. At the same time, those working to support this system are becoming slaves carrying heavy tax burdens. Local tax burdens have also grown rapidly. Schools and fighting crime are two of the major costs of local governments.

"Recently your Surgeon General said on national TV that we have taught our children what to do in the front seat of our cars and now we have to teach them what to do in the back seat. Statistics would indicate otherwise. High teen accident rates show that you have not adequately taught your children how to be careful and caring sober drivers. High teen pregnancies and AIDS show that your children have learned to practice their sex education in the back seats of their cars. You should have been teaching them the commandments of the Bible not to have premarital sex."

Sonny paused and then he said, "Your health, Mrs. Us, is dependent on the spiritual, moral, and physical health of your people. Spiritual health comes from a close relationship with the God of creation, and has little to do with religious activity. Lately, your media have been talking a lot about the "religious right." They overlook the fact that many of them are part of a very vocal *religious left* that preaches the doctrine of instant self gratification.

"Your overall health is also dependent upon your financial condition." Reaching for his briefcase, he pulled out two folders and said, "I recently stopped by a high school where they were emphasizing excellence in science, math, and Bible-based principles of real-life learning. The social studies teacher had given her class a project to study your financial health. She gave her class your charts that Nurse Trustworthy showed you back in the hospital, and a copy of the government published book, *Statistical Abstracts of the United States*. She showed them your spending habits as seen in Chart 1, and then divided her class into two groups. Each of the groups was asked to choose a leader, and given a different set of instructions.

"Andy's group (A) was asked to assume that your present spending increases continue to the year 2000. In addition, they were to assume that the proposed universal health insurance plan, financed largely by employers, was adopted. Betty's group (B) was asked to develop a plan that if implemented, would balance the budget by the end of the century. Both groups were asked to provide information on what they did and why they did it. Here are the results."

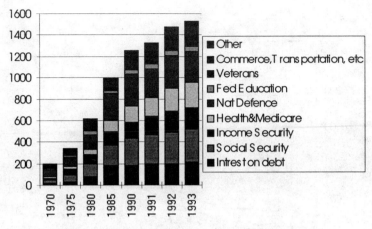

Legend:
- Other
- Commerce, Transportation, etc
- Veterans
- Fed Education
- Nat Defence
- Health&Medicare
- Income Security
- Social Security
- Intrest on debt

CHART 1. FEDERAL GOVERNMENT SPENDING

FINANCIAL PROJECTIONS FOR MRS. Us BY GROUP A
Assumed:
1. Spending continues to increase at its present rate of growth
2. Continued foreign military involvement
3. Added health care expenditures
4. Added tax rate increases with regressive income yields

From chart 2 you can see that:
1. Federal income increases only slightly due to industrial layoffs.
2. Federal expenditures increase significantly as the year 2000 approaches due in part to increased social programs, health care, crime, and increasing debt interest charges.
3. The National Debt is seen to reach in excess of 12 trillion dollars by the year 2000.
4. By 1996 the interest payments reach over 35% of the Federal income, and by 1998 are almost 60%.

It is clear, Mrs. Us, that if your administration and Congress continue on this course that you will be bankrupt in three to five years.

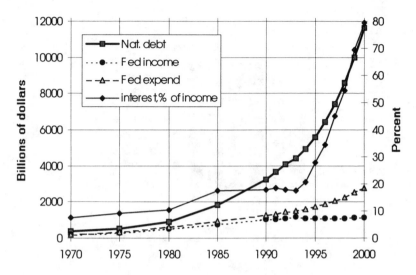

CHART 2. FINANCIAL PROJECTIONS FOR MRS. US BY GROUP A.

FINANCIAL PROJECTIONS FOR MRS. Us BY GROUP B

Objective: Balance budget by the year 2000 (see results in Chart 3.)

Background:

1. Group B looked at early projections by group A, and could see that significant reduction in spending must start **very soon.**
2. They examined Chart 4 of Chapter 1, and the federal budget where they saw that in 1960 federal spending on education was 968 million, and SAT scores were 970. By 1980 federal spending on education had risen to almost 32 billion and SAT scores had dropped to 885.
3. They saw that the costs due to violence, drugs, bank scandals, and health care are growing very fast, and concluded that unless violence, drugs, and corruption are curbed by a spiritual revival, the budget will not be balanced.

Assumed:

1. Nation-wide revival, return to "One Nation under God" (this is essential if crime, violence and fraud costs are to be reduced).

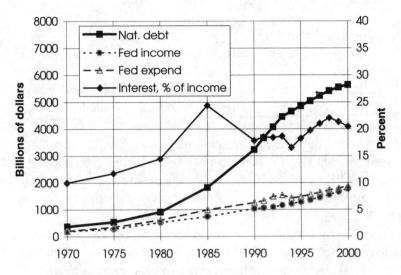

CHART 3. FINANCIAL PROJECTIONS FOR MRS. US BY GROUP B.

2. Major amounts of the "right flux" (see chapter 2) are added.
3. Truth and trust restored along with justice in the courts.
4. Reduced Federal spending by:
   a. Drastically reducing the federal Department of Education spending (return schools to the parents and local school boards).
   b. Having a spiritual revival which will result in less violence, reduced crime-fighting costs. (Parents will be taught the importance of teaching children from God's Instruction Book so that they will not become criminals).
   c. Reducing federal funding of medical spending.
   d. Reducing the size of EPA and OSHA. (A balance must be restored between environmental and economic needs).
   e. Reducing unemployment spending.
5. Reduced state and local government spending, (less spending on excessive administration).
6. Expanded research and development of new products, and increasing industrial productivity.

7. Expanded use of renewable energy sources.

Additional requirements:
1. Employment levels must be raised by increasing incentives to work (for both employees and employers).
2. Reduce incentives to live off welfare or unemployment.
3. Reduce the legal hazards that face doctors, hospitals, businesses and all citizens.

The results of these changes are seen in Chart 3.

Federal spending is reduced in 1994. Federal income starts to rise as small and large businesses are freed from excessive tax, regulatory and legal burdens. Income and expenditures become nearly equal by the year 2000.

Mrs. Us studied the two reports in silence for several minutes, and then exclaimed, "Sonny, it looks like my budget **can** be balanced, but it sure will take some changed hearts to get my people working together!" There were a few more moments of silence as Mrs. Us looked back at Chart 2. Then she said, "If we don't start soon, it looks like at best I'm in for some very hard times." Then she said softly, "If we don't start soon, I may not even *make it* to the year 2000!"

Sonny reached over and put his arms around Mrs. Us and said, "Many in your churches are being told to turn from selfish and sinful ways. If they start reading and studying their Instruction Book and turn to God with all their hearts, He will hear. He will enable them to reach out to those in need, to those who as yet have not accepted their Gift of a new heart and eternal life from their Creator. As your people return to the God of your Founding Fathers and Mothers, He will heal your land."

"Thank, you Sonny," Mrs. Us said as she kissed him good-bye. "I'm going to give this message to my people, yes, and to my President, my Congress, and my Judges.

CHAPTER NOTES

There *is* hope for Mrs. Us if we listen to God's call to turn to Him. John Quincy Adams wrote this: "*Remember, democracy never lasts long. It soon wastes, exhausts, murders itself. There never was a democracy yet that did not commit suicide. It is vain to say that democracy is less vain, less proud, less selfish, less ambitious than aristocracy or monarchy.... Those passions are the same in all men, under all forms of simple government, and when **unchecked**, produce the same effects of fraud, violence, and cruelty* [emphases added]." One of the key words in this statement is **unchecked**. We are seeing the growth of fraud, violence, and cruelty in our country as a result of removing the boundaries God has given in His Instruction Book. These are the boundaries which keep the passions of men and women in check.

A new social experiment was started in the United States during the 1960s when the Bible was outlawed in our schools and government. This action, which is clearly contrary to the first amendment of the U.S. Constitution, has borne its bitter fruit. President Clinton was right when he said that America needed a change. The change that we need is to return to having the passions of men and women checked. This can be done by following the instructions such as are given in the Bible—instructions that were adhered to by our Founding Mothers and Fathers.

The prophet Isaiah gave this message to the people of Israel at a time when they had turned away from God, such as is occurring in America today. "*... Your hands are full of bloodshed. Wash yourselves, make yourselves clean, remove the evil of your deeds from My sight. Cease to do evil, Learn to do good; Seek justice, Reprove the ruthless, defend the orphan, Plead for the widow. Come now and let us reason together says the LORD, though your sins are as scarlet, they shall be as white as snow, Though they be red like crimson, they shall be like wool. If you consent and obey, you will eat the best of the land, but if you refuse and rebel, you will be devoured by the sword.*"[4]

Now is the time to consent to and obey God's commandments. If we do, He will heal our land.

[1] Deuteronomy 32:28, NEB

[2] Burkett, Larry, *What Ever Happened to the American Dream?*, Moody Press, Chicago, 1993

[3] John 13:34, NASB

[4] Isaiah 1:15-20, NASB

CHAPTER 6

MRS. US AND THE AMAZING GIFT

FREE TO CHOOSE

ER HEART FELT HEAVY AS SHE LOOKED OUT HER WINDOW. THE VIEW OF THE HARBOR SEEMED TO FADE, AND HER VISION REACHED OUT OVER HER VAST LAND AS IT HAD BEEN IN YEARS past. Ships in her harbor where unloading new arrivals. Beyond was the vast metropolis of New York with its parks and skyscrapers. Then her view shifted to her beautiful Capital City with its marble buildings, parks, and monuments of the past. Next, Mrs. Us saw Atlanta, Miami, Chicago, St. Louis, and finally Los Angeles with the blue Pacific waters of her west coast. In her mind she saw the beauty that had been theirs in years past. Children were playing in the parks, and she could almost feel the throb of business and industry.

Then her view spread out over these same cities as they are today. The scene was much different. Mothers were afraid to let their children play in the parks. In many cities, children dreaded going to school or even to walk down the street for fear of violence. She saw innocent children lying slain in the streets. Yes, she knew that there had been difficult times in the past, but never before like this. Children shooting children, even in the schools. Motorists were being killed by thugs on the freeways, and now even on country roads.

Mrs. Us knew that this must be stopped if she was to regain her former health. Her mind flashed back to Chart 1[1] that Nurse Trustworthy had shown her when she was in the Washington hospital. Violent crime indeed had risen dramatically over the past three decades, but now even children have become violent killers of other children, yes, and even of

77

their teachers! What is the root cause of all this violence, she wondered, and how can it be stopped?

Last night on TV she saw a government official proposing a ban on guns as a way to stop the killing. She knew that there were too many guns in the hands of children as well as criminals. However, she also knew that back in the early days of her country almost all families had several guns for hunting within easy reach and yet children were not shooting children or their teachers in the schools. Families then had a father at home who taught the children how to handle firearms safely. Children were taught God's commandments: *"Honor thy father and thy mother," "Thou shalt not kill,"* and *"Thou shalt not steal."*

"That must be it," she exclaimed out loud, "Children had fathers and mothers at home who taught them God's commandments."

She heard a knock on her door and when she opened it, there was her favorite nurse who gave her a big hug. "I was just thinking about you and my charts that you showed me back in the Washington, DC, hospital!" Mrs. Us exclaimed. "I keep hoping that there will be a reduction in violent crime, but it just seems to be getting worse."

"I know," Nurse Trustworthy replied. "I have come to tell you why. During an earlier visit, when you were in the Washington hospital, I brought a white-robed Messenger from the Central Record Department to see you. He reminded you that each year the Creator has sent you many souls to care for. He also told you that with each soul there was a very special Gift box placed in layaway until claimed. Each soul is free to choose whether to accept or to reject this Gift. Dr. Truth will be coming to tell you more about this special Gift and why it is so important to you and your health. Before he comes, he asked me to tell you what else came with each soul."

PHYSICAL LIFE ON LOAN

"With each soul comes the gift of a most amazing body. Actually this gift of physical life is more like a temporary loan. It is yours to enjoy but not to keep! The duration of this loan is indefinite. For some it lasts only a few months, and for others it may last for over 100 years.

"The human body is one of the most amazing designs of all time. It functions well on a wide variety of fuels, and enjoys consuming them. It has a wide variety of built-in sensors, which in conjunction with a fantastic computer system in the command and control center, enable it to perform an almost endless variety of tasks. Although primarily designed for functioning on land, men and women function well (with the aid of machines designed by them) in water, in the air, and yes, now even in space as far away as the moon. With proper clothing, they can function well over an extreme range of temperatures from the sub-zero Arctic to inside burning buildings.

"One of the tasks the Creator gave to Adam and Eve is described in the first chapter of His Instruction Book. '*So God created man in his own image, in the image of God created he them. And God blessed them, and God said unto them, Be fruitful, and multiply, and replenish the earth....*'[2] Like most of the tasks the Creator designed, this one brings pleasure, accomplishment, and responsibility. The Chief Designer, when he was here on special assignment, said this to a group gathered near the Jordan River. '*Have you not read, that He who created them from the beginning made them male and female, and said, for this cause a man shall leave his father and mother, and shall cleave to his wife, and the two shall become one flesh? Consequently they are no more two, but one flesh. What therefore God has joined together, let no man separate.*'[3]

"Unlike most other creatures in nature, human babies and children require a rather long period of care and instruction. This is best accomplished when the mother and father cooperate and share in the tasks of parenting the new generation. To do this well requires a great deal of time, wisdom, and loving devotion. When properly done the rewards are great."

At this point the nurse looked up and in an unusually stern voice said, "Mrs. Us, this is one of your major problems. A large number of your citizens were never parented or properly instructed how to live in a free and self-governing society. Too many children are having children! They lack the knowledge and often the means to raise this new generation. Instead, many (even some that have become adults) are still children who have no knowledge of God and His ways, or of right and wrong. The computer hardware of their brains is up and running, but the essential software and programming required to produce happy, useful, and productive members of society is missing."

Mrs. Us, who had been listening carefully, exclaimed, "I know that many of my children and youths are in deep trouble, and this is making me ill! How did this happen? What must be done to fix it?"

STEPS TO MORAL DECAY AND VIOLENCE

Nurse Trustworthy replied, "I'll tell you how it came about, but when Dr. Truth comes to visit you he will tell you how it can be cured. There were four root causes that led to your present violence:

- Parents became too involved in pursuing money and pleasure and did not parent their children.
- Social activists got into your schools and welfare systems, discarded the Bible, and taught that there is no right or wrong.
- Childhood rebellion was not punished and became criminal behavior.
- Justice was not carried out quickly and violent offenders were often released in a short time to continue their life of violence.

Solomon described the effect of the fourth cause almost 3,000 years ago. "*Because sentence against an evil work is not executed speedily, therefore the heart of the sons of men is fully set in them to do evil.*"[4] Children learn quickly. They see murderers either escape justice or, if imprisoned, back out in a few years to murder again.

"Now before Dr. Truth arrives I must tell you more about the human body, soul, and spirit. God has given each person the right of choice. He tells us what is right and what is wrong. He tells us the consequences of our choices, but leaves us free to choose.

"The body given to each soul has a number of senses. The primary senses are sight, sound, smell, taste, and touch. The eyes respond to electromagnetic energy with wavelengths in the 0.4 to 0.8 micro meter region. This is near the center of the radiation spectrum of our sun. The eyes are extremely sensitive, and yet can adapt to a very wide range of illumination. They also are equipped to pre-process images for potential danger. The ears respond to pressure waves. They also are amazingly sensitive over a wide frequency range. They can discriminate between different sounds such as the voices of your friends or different musical instruments. They also provide information on the direction of sound sources. In humans, the sense of smell is not as sensitive as in some animals and insects. The human nose, well placed right above the mouth, does have a unique ability to detect a new odor which may signal danger, but it soon becomes desensitized as one adapts to a new smell environment. Taste is closely related to smell as it also provides warning of dangerous food, and brings pleasure to eating. Touch provides warning of danger from sharp, hot, or cold objects. It also provides pleasure such as the reassurance of a friend's handshake or the embrace of a dear friend. In combination, the senses provide the soul with a wide variety of sensations, ranging from pleasure to pain. Unfortunately, there are also the sensations of anguish and despair. These can result when people—rather than loving their neighbors—let greed and hatred in their souls and spirits produce violent acts against their fellow humans. This is seen throughout the world.

"It is in the realm of sensations that a person can become addicted. Some addictions, such as desiring good food and exercise, are good for the individual. On the other hand there are practices that yield to sensations which become addictions that are disastrous to the individual and those around him. These types of addictions, Mrs. Us, are what makes solving your problems so difficult. For example, if a person becomes addicted to drugs, he may become enslaved and often will do anything, including theft and murder, to satisfy his addiction. If your parents had been raising their children properly and teaching them God's commandments, you would not have your present problems. Once a person becomes addicted to a life of crime and violence, simple instructions are not enough to turn him from that life-style.

"Your government is spending vast sums of money to try and solve the addictions of your people with very little success. One of the reasons for their lack of success is that those running the programs are not aware of the inter-workings of the body, soul, and spirit as designed by the Creator. This knowledge, contained in the Bible, has been largely overlooked by the present generation. The writer of the letter to the Hebrews put it this way, '*For the word of God is active and sharper than any two-edged sword, and piercing as far as the division of soul and spirit, of both joints and marrow, and able to judge the thoughts and intentions of the heart.*'[5] Many of today's problems are the result of souls driven by a spirit of greed or hate received from Arch Enemy instead of a spirit of love received from God and His Word."

"What actually is the difference between soul and spirit?" Mrs. Us interjected.

"That's a good question," her nurse replied. "The Hebrews and Greeks probably realized the difficulty of discerning the difference much easier than we. In these languages the word for soul has it's roots in the word for a soft breath while the word for spirit relates to a strong breath. Many times it is hard to say if a breath is hard or soft. Likewise, it is often difficult for men to discern between right and wrong. It's here that the Bible stands as a reliable standard of what's right and what's wrong.

"The soul of man is that emotional part that desires to be pleased but can be displeased. David said, '*my soul is bowed down*,'[6] and then, referring to the Good Shepherd, he said '*He restores my soul*.'[7] Job said, '*My soul is weary of my life*.'[8] Jesus, before He went to the cross, said, '*My soul is exceedingly sorrowful*.'[9] The soul appears to be related more to feelings, and perhaps more passive than active.

"The spirit is primarily active, but can be grieved. We read that, '*the Spirit of God moved upon the face of the waters*.'[10] We also are told that the Lord formed the spirit of man within him.[11] A person can have a loving or a gentle spirit, while there are others who have a hateful and destructive spirit. Man's spirit directs the activities of his body, and can be influenced for evil by a spirit from Arch Enemy, or for good by the Creator's Holy Spirit."

At this point Nurse Trustworthy got up and said, "I have to leave now, but Dr. Truth will tell you more about the workings of body, soul, and spirit when he comes to see you tomorrow morning." She put her arms around Mrs. Us and said, "I love you, Mrs. Us. I hope that you and your doctors and specialists in Washington will make the right choice."

Then she kissed her patient good-bye and hurried down the stairs.

After supper, Mrs. Us sat looking out over the harbor while her mind mulled over all that her nurse had told her. "How fortunate I am," she thought, "to have a nurse who loves and cares for me and is trying so hard to help me get better. Now I must get some rest and be ready for Dr. Truth in the morning."

Dr. TRUTH AND THE MOST AMAZING GIFT

Dr. Truth arrived on time and greeted his patient with a cheery, "Good morning, Mrs. Us. You are looking better today." He pulled up a chair next to her's, grasped her hand, and started to take her pulse. From the unusually long silence, Mrs. Us sensed that the Doctor had something very important to tell her.

"Doctor," she asked, "why is this Gift that the Almighty is offering to each soul so important to them, and to me? The wonderful body given to each of them seems like all a person could ask for. Why bother to pick up this Gift?"

Doctor Truth, in his deep but gentle voice, replied, "I know that many of your people are thinking just that. Arch Enemy is doing his best to prevent souls from picking up their Gift. For some he keeps them busy pursuing happiness. Some he convinces that the Gift is really not important, and then he hides it from others. If people only knew the importance of the Gift, and all the fringe benefits that it brings, there would be a rush of people to pick up the many unclaimed Gifts.

"Nurse Trustworthy has told you about the gift, or really the loan, of physical life that each of your citizens has received. This is for many a highly valued possession as they enjoy life and their surroundings. Unfortunately, there are also millions on the earth, and yes, in your land, who are not enjoying life. For some, who have not picked up their Gift, life is a round of emptiness. For others life is full of fear or hunger.

"The same Creator God who has given out these loans of physical life is making a most amazing gift offer to all those possessing physical life. The gift of eternal life is part of this Gift package that comes with each soul. This Gift which has been bought and placed in layaway for each soul to claim is a true gift, not a loan. God has left each person *free to choose*, either to reject or to claim their Gift. Once claimed it is theirs to keep forever. Like most gifts, and unlike physical life, it must be claimed or accepted before it becomes theirs.

"First I will tell you how each soul can claim his or her Gift. Next I'll describe some of the details of the Gift and what comes with each Gift packet. Then I'll tell you about the cost and price of the Gift. Finally I will tell you why it is so important to you, Mrs. Us, for your citizens to claim their Gifts."

Claiming The Gift

"Fortunately, this is the easiest part of the Gift. Many things made by the Creator are profoundly simple to use or employ, but are extremely complex in their nature. Water is a good example. Drinking it is easy. Describing it is much more complex, as whole books have been written on the properties of water. There is light water and heavy water, liquid water, ice, steam, distilled water, and, yes, plenty of salt water. All have their own unique physical and chemical properties. It is interesting that the provider of the Gift described it as living water to the woman at Jacob's well. He told her, '*Whoever drinks of the water that I shall give him shall never thirst; but the water that I shall give him shall become in him a well of water springing up to eternal life.*'[12]

"You see, accepting the Gift is as easy as accepting a glass of water. It takes an act of your will (your spirit) to accept, and yes faith to believe that it is good to drink. Jesus also described claiming the Gift this way, '*He who believes in the Son has eternal life. ...*'[13] *Believes in* has the force in the original language of being persuaded to place your faith in (into) Jesus as the Son of God. Jesus is the One who purchased this most expensive of all Gifts. He paid for it when He allowed His life's blood to be shed as He hung on the cross some 2,000 years ago!

"Some of your souls have not picked up their Gift since they have not been persuaded that it is real or that they need it. Urge them to accept it today as this is a limited-time offer good only before death or the return of the Chief Designer to claim His bride, the church—whichever occurs first. The reality of the Gift is best discovered by reading about it in the Bible. It always pays to go to the source.

Another proof of reality is seen in the amazing change the Gift can produce in the lives of those receiving it. Now let me tell you more about this Gift."

Details of the Amazing Gift

"The centerpiece of the Gift is **eternal life**. The apostle Paul, writing to the Romans put it this way: '*For the wages of sin is death, but the gift of God is eternal life through Jesus Christ our Lord.*'[14] This Gift is much more than a life insurance policy that becomes effective on physical death. Upon reception of the Gift, God gives each soul new life which Jesus described as being "born again." The part of a person's spirit which died in Adam is made alive again in Jesus Christ. God's Spirit of love can once again react with our spirit. The natural spirit which seeks only to please its own soul now can be influenced by the Holy Spirit. Such a person now desires to please God and show His love to others. The new birth does not require a long training period to change a person's life. Although there may be a time of preparation before a person is ready to accept the Gift, the new birth is instantaneous. Prior to the new birth, Arch Enemy was easily able to influence a person to hate and even to kill."

"Are there other changes involved?" Mrs. Us asked.

"Yes, there are," Doctor Truth replied. "Listen to this. '*Therefore having been justified by faith, we have peace with God through our Lord Jesus Christ,*'[15] A person becomes justified and now has peace with God and is free from coming judgment. '*He who believes in the Son has everlasting life, and he who does not believe the Son shall not see life, but the wrath of God abides on him.*'[16] There are many wonderful things that come with the Gift. Unfortunately, some persons never look past the first part of the wrapping paper to discover what else is in this amazing Gift package.

"Back in the years when the Almighty was sending you many souls by ship, there was a couple that sold their home in Europe and bought one-way steamship tickets to America. Since they had very little extra money, they took a large package of bread and cheese with them which they ate in their cabin. On the last day before landing in New York, the aroma from the bountiful meal in the dining room was just too much for them to resist. They asked the steward if there was some way that they could get in to eat with the others enjoying the feast. The steward asked to look at their tickets and then informed them that they were entitled to all the meals being served for the whole passage.

"Unfortunately, many who have accepted God's Gift of eternal life have been living on bread and cheese when they could have been enjoying the bounty of God's provision for the rest of life's journey. One of the most important aspects to you, Mrs. Us, is that persons living under the control of God's Spirit become faithful and truthful citizens. This will reduce both white-collar and violent crime. There will be a direct saving to you of billions of dollars as well as indirect saving of many more billions resulting from better health for your citizens."

Need for the Amazing Gift

"You were told earlier how the Creator formed Adam from the dust of the earth and then breathed into him the breath of life, where the Hebrew word for life has a dual form. Adam was given a living, physical body that related to his surroundings and brought pleasure to his soul. He was also given a living spirit that was alive and could communicate freely with his Creator. The Almighty Creator told Adam and Eve that they were free to choose what to do and what to eat except that they should not eat of the tree of the knowledge of good and evil. They were also told that the day they ate of it they would die. You know what happened—how they ate, and that very day they lost their *spiritual* life (direct access to God) and started the process of *physical* death. Breaking God's rules is called sin, and the penalty for sin is death. When Adam sinned, The Almighty could not say, "Let's forget it," and give man another chance or He would be breaking His own word and His own rules. Sin required the death penalty; someone had to pay!

"Since Adam lost his spiritual life before his sons were born, he could not pass it on to them or to the present generations. The Almighty knew this would happen, and had already made plans to meet this need. This Gift of God is sort of like a kit provided to correct a defect caused by Adam making the wrong choice."

"I see!" Mrs. Us exclaimed. "Every soul sent to me by the Almighty has inherited a congenital defect from Adam that needs to be corrected."

"Yes," the doctor answered, "that is true, and in addition to having this defect passed on from Adam, each soul has also broken one or more of God's commands. *'For all have sinned and come short of the glory of God.'*[17]

"Now I can see why each soul needs the Gift if they want to be freed from the sentence of death," Mrs. Us said. "But is it really true that this Gift is being offered free to every soul, and how much did the Provider have to pay to be able to make this offer?"

Cost and Price

"Sometimes we use the terms *cost* and *price* loosely, as though they are the same," Doctor Truth replied. "Actually there is a great difference. Cost is what it takes to produce an item, while price is what it's sold for. Usually the price in a store is several times the actual cost. This Gift is much different. It's cost was great but the price is free to all who accept the Gift!

"God the Father had to see His Son that He loved dearly suffer and die to be able to offer the Gift. The Gift was actually purchased by the blood of Jesus. The price to you is simply to believe and receive the Gift. *'But as many as received Him, to them He gave the right to become the children of God, to those who believe in His name.'*[18]

"Although the Gift is given free to each soul who receives it, there is a cost involved after it's received. To fully enjoy all the provisions of the Gift, the soul of man needs to turn from putting self-gratification first to putting God first. Solomon expressed it this way, *'My son, give me your heart, and let your eyes observe my ways.'*[19] When this is done a person's soul experiences a lasting joy and satisfaction far greater than any pleasures this world can give. The greatest fulfillment for man is living in harmony and at peace with the Creator of the universe."

The Importance of the Gift to Mrs. Us

"Thank you, Doctor, for explaining the Gift to me," Mrs. Us said. "I can see why every soul needs and should pick up his or her Gift right away, but how does this affect my health?"

Choosing his words carefully, Doctor Truth replied, "When Nurse Trustworthy spoke to you yesterday, it was clear to both of you that crime and violence has become one of your major problems. It is important that violent criminals be punished quickly and with justice. In some areas this may require more police to protect your citizens. Also needed is a judicial system that dispenses justice quickly and surely.

"The real solution, however, is not just more police and more jails. Over the past three decades, the number of your citizens seeking instant self-gratification has grown at an alarming rate. A person who has not learned God's commandments and how to live in a self-governing society can easily fall into a life of violence and crime. Once a person is programmed into a life of crime and violence he cannot easily be turned back into a loving, productive member of society. A radical transformation is required. This can be accomplished by the life-transforming power of the new birth, the amazing Gift of God."

Dr. Truth got up to leave and as he grasped her hand in both of his, he said in a stern but kind voice, "Mrs. Us, your health, and even your survival, depends on getting this life-transforming news of the most amazing Gift out to your citizens. Tell them that they are *free to choose.* Urge them to *make the right choice.*"

CHAPTER NOTES

We live in an era of amazing technical accomplishments. New energy sources and communication systems have the potential of raising the standard of living in our nation. All this will profit us nothing if we lose our own souls. If the rising tide of violence, crime, and lack of trust continues, and the Right Flux of God's love is not soon added, Mrs. Us's melting pot may soon boil over. If this happens, new technology, money, police, and laws will not be able to stop disaster.

God loves every one of Mrs. Us's citizens and wants the best for them. His Spirit in them will make them loving, faithful, and trustworthy neighbors. If you haven't yet accepted your amazing Gift from God, now is the best time to do so. He wants you to come to him just as you are.

The Gift does not promise perfect health or instant wealth, but the Giver of the Gift promises, "*I will never leave you nor forsake you.*"[20] Life still will have trials and temptations, but now the Creator of the universe is there to hold your hand and guide you through the dangerous canyons of life.

---

[1] From Chapter 1, "Mrs. Us Is Ill"

[2] Genesis 1:27-28, KJV

[3] Matthew 19:4-6, NASB

[4] Ecclesiastes 8:11, KJV

[5] Hebrews 4:12, NASB

[6] Psalm 57:6, KJV

[7] Psalm 23:3, NKJV

[8] Job 10:1, KJV

[9] Matthew 26:38, NKJV

[10] Genesis 1:2, KJV

[11] Zechariah 12:1, KJV

[12] John 4:14 NASB

[13] John 3:36 NASB

[14] Romans 6:23 KJV

Us and the Amazing Gift

[15] Romans 5:1, NKJV
[16] John 3:36, NKJV
[17] Romans 3:23, KJV
[18] John 1:12, NKJV
[19] Proverbs 23:26, NKJV
[20] Hebrews 13:5, NKJV

90

CHAPTER 7

LETTERS FROM MRS. US

WEIGHED IN THE BALANCES

SITTING IN HER LIVING ROOM, MRS. US WAS PONDERING THE EVENTS OF THE YEAR 1993 THAT WAS FAST DRAWING TO A CLOSE. SHE RECALLED THAT THIS HAD BEEN THE YEAR OF THE *BIG* RAINS AND floods. Then she remembered the recent years of the *big* winds, the *big* fires in Berkeley and L. A., and the *big* quake in San Francisco, and wondered what *big* disasters to expect in the coming year. She could not help but believe that she was being weighed in God's balances, and wondered if she was seeing the handwriting on the wall. Would the hand that wrote, MENE MENE TEKEL UPHARSIN, in Daniel's time, write to her, TEKEL, "you are weighed in the balances and found wanting"? Or even worse would her message include MENE, "God has numbered your kingdom and finished it"?

Then she wondered about all the crime and violence in her land. Tears came to her eyes as she thought of all the mothers whose children had been killed in the past year in her streets and schools. "What can I do to stop this carnage and to improve the quality of life of my citizens?" she wondered.

"I know," she exclaimed! "I must write letters to my doctors in Washington and tell them what I think they should do!" While she wondered where to start, she realized that something else had to be done. "First," she said, "I'm going to sit right down and write myself a letter. I have to change as well as my doctors before things will get better."

From the Desk of Mrs. Us

To all of Us

Dear Friends,

Before we can regain our health, the following real changes must be made.

If you are one of Us who has claimed the Gift, you as well as I must live as truly God-fearing people. We must read and study God's Instruction Book. We must ask God's forgiveness for any evil in our lives and start living as He directs. We must show the love of God to fellow Christians as well as to all those around us. This must take precedence over seeking great economic gain for ourselves or trying to survive coming economic hard times. We must get the news of the amazing Gift out to all.

If you are one of Us who is burdened down with cares and seemingly insurmountable problems, I urge you to accept this most valuable Gift from the One who says, *"Come to me all you that labor and are heavy laden and I will give you rest."* Matthew 11:28.

If you are one of Us who is lonely, God loves you. He really wants you as a friend. He wants you to accept His Gift. He will always be *"A friend that will never leave you."* Hebrews 13:5.

If you are one of Us who is pursuing instant gratification to try and find happiness, be assured that real lasting joy is only found in the One who loves you and is offering you the amazing Gift *"that your joy might be full."* John 5:11.

If you are one of Us who is behind bars, there is One who desires to set you free from sin and your past. If you ask, He will give you a new heart. Then when you are released, He can enable you to become a happy and productive member of society. "*If the Son shall make you free, you shall be free indeed.*" John 8:32.

With much love,
Mrs. Us

Just as she finished the first letter, there was a knock at her door, and she heard Sonny call, "Are you home, Mrs. Us?"

"Do come in, Sonny," she replied.

Sonny put his briefcase down, gave Mrs. Us a hug, and sat down next to her. "Headquarters told me that you would be writing letters to Washington. They also gave me material to enclose in each of your letters." Reaching into his briefcase he took out three enclosures and handed them to Mrs. Us. "There is one for your President, one for your Congress, and one for your Justices and their associates.

"Thank you, Sonny," she said, " I'll be sure to enclose these with the letters when I send them. By the way, how are things going in the other melting pots around the world?"

After a moment's hesitation Sonny replied, "It seems on the surface that some places, such as Ireland, may have a chance of doing better. However, there is still much violence in the world. You thought a year ago that there was to be a big peace dividend, and started down-sizing your military. Actually the dangers are still great."

Looking for a more cheery subject, Mrs. Us said, "Sonny, I have been wondering, how you can tell if a person has accepted the Gift?"

Sonny replied, "The Almighty is the only one who knows for sure. There is, however, a good test. When a person accepts the Gift, God's Spirit in him produces fruit. '*But the fruit of the Spirit is love, joy, peace, patience, kindness, goodness, faithfulness, gentleness, self-control....*'[1] You see, when your citizens have God's Spirit in them, and they let Him direct their lives, they can be trusted and will make good workers and good neighbors.

"When the Chief Designer was here on special assignment, the average person saw just another man. Those who got to know Him soon realized that He was different. The blind were made to see, the deaf to hear, the wind and the waves obeyed His voice. They saw Him walk on water, they saw Him die, they saw Him live again, and they saw Him ascend into the clouds.

"The prophet was given the secret of this unique Man when he wrote, over 700 years before the day of His birth, '*For unto us a child is born, unto us a Son is given....*'[2] This Man was not another son of Adam. Here was a special body, soul and spirit that had not inherited the genetic defect from Adam. A child was *born* to Mary, but the eternal Son of God was *given* to us.

"There is another secret that not all who have accepted their Gift have learned. Paul wrote this to a self-seeking civilization much like yours, Mrs. Us: '*His purpose in dying for all was that men, when still in life, should cease to live for themselves, and should live for Him who for their sake died and was raised to life.*'[3] Jesus told this secret for real life to His disciples when He told them, '*Whoever shall lose his life for my sake, shall save it.*'[4] Much of your problem, Mrs. Us, is that many of your people are trying hard to find life by seeking instant self-gratification, and are losing their lives trying." Sonny had barely finished when his beeper went off. "Mrs. Us, I have to leave on an urgent call!" he exclaimed. Then he kissed her on the forehead and called out as he started for the door, "Have a good day, Mrs. Us, and be sure to get your letters mailed soon."

Mrs. Us reached for more paper and started to write.

From the Desk of Mrs. Us

The White House
1600 Pennsylvania Ave.

Dear Mr. President,
    You are faced with many complex problems. Many of these are the result of actions by those who have preceded you in the Washington scene. Be assured that you have

---

been placed where you are by the Almighty Creator. "*The Most High rules in the kingdom of men, and gives it to whomever he chooses.*" Daniel 4:32, NKJV

The future of our country depends on the actions of all of Us as well as on your decisions. We still live in a world with dangers from without as well as from within.

We are pleased to see that you are giving more attention to our serious problem of violent crime, but I would remind you that outlawing guns assures that only outlaws will have guns. Criminal behavior must be punished so that crime does not pay. For the real long-time solution, I suggest that you call in Dr. Truth for consultation on the importance of having loving families that produce loving and law-abiding citizens.

One of the potential dangers in a self-governing society is when minorities are able to force their own self-interests on the country. This becomes a serious problem when these self-interests are contrary to Almighty God's commands and put the whole nation at risk. I was disappointed in your yielding to the clamor of a self-seeking minority that is trying to set up a new god of instant self-gratification in my country.

I am concerned with the safety of all my citizens. I advise you to listen to the advice of those who have been running my military for years, and to stop risking my safety and reducing the morale of my military to please the self-interest of a few.

Mr. President, God has given you a healthy body and many talents. You are in a place of grave responsibility. Like Belshazzar of old, the Almighty places rulers as well as nations in the balances. You, as well as I, are in His balances. Two of your predecessors, Washington and Lincoln, were men who read, studied, and went to God's Instruction Book for advice. They were not found wanting, and are remembered as our two greatest presidents.

There are changes that you, Mr. President, as well as I must make if we are not to be found wanting when the Almighty next reads His balances. I respectfully request that you, as well as all of us, read and heed the Almighty's Instruction Book. Do not think that simply associating with some religious leaders will help. God is not impressed with an external image!

When Jonah warned Nineveh of coming destruction, the people and the king repented and God spared the city. God is warning us, and if we repent, turn from evil, and ask God's forgiveness for disobeying His commands, I am sure that I will regain my health.

Sincerely Yours,
Mrs. Us

Enclosure *"Blessed be God's name from age to age, for all wisdom and power are his. He changes seasons and times; he deposes kings and sets them up; he gives wisdom to the wise and all their store of knowledge to men who know; he reveals deep mysteries"* (Daniel 2:21-23, NEB)

From the Desk of Mrs. Us

Capitol Hill
Dear Members of Congress,

Some of you are trying to find solutions to my ill health. For this I thank you. Over the years many of you have not been paying the right attention to my finances, and are now placing on me a burden of too high taxes. You have been conducting your business in a manner that often hides the truth from the rest of us.

It is time for many of you to stop seeking your own self-interest and start representing me. The Almighty will hold each of you accountable for any evil in your lives. I will hold those of you accountable who have neglected my best interests to serve your own interests or those of some special-interest pressure group.

It is time for you to re-establish truth and integrity in your operations. This can only be done if you start consulting with Dr. Truth and start reading and heeding the Almighty's Instruction Book.

If my health fails, do not think that you will escape. Your provisions for generous retirements (far better than for the rest of us) will be of no value if I become terminal. To prevent this, you must set your house in order and work to help me regain my health. All of us will be watching to see your progress in these matters.

Don't be misled into taking away our freedom to choose our doctors and force all to pay for a bureaucratic nightmare of old Soviet-style health insurance.

Good health comes from good health habits, good food and freedom from worry. Many of my citizens are sick from having to work long hours to pay burdensome taxes and worrying about all the changing laws coming from Washington. All that you do to improve my health will be greatly appreciated.

Sincerely Yours,
Mrs. Us

Enclosure
   "Righteousness exalts a nation, but sin is a disgrace to any people." (Proverbs 14:34, NASB)

From the Desk of Mrs. Us

Justices of the US Supreme Court
Dear Justices,

You have been given the responsibility of interpreting the Constitution of the United States, my birth certificate. In years past we functioned as one nation under God. Several decades ago, you were persuaded by a small vocal minority to try and remove God from an important part of our nation, my schools. This has had disastrous results in decreased proficiency of my students, increased teen pregnancy, social diseases, and increased violence and crime in my streets.

Your predecessors in my early days were well aware of the importance of self-consistent and stable laws. The Almighty has allowed each of you to be placed where you are. You have a grave responsibility to arrive at rulings which are consistent with the original intent of my Constitution. Be assured that some day you will stand before the Chief Justice of the universe to account for your decisions. I urge each of you to read and heed God's Instruction Book so that you can make rulings that will help me return to my former health.

Sincerely Yours,
Mrs. Us

Enclosure
"*And I saw the dead small and great, standing before God, and the books were opened. And another book was opened, which is the Book of Life. And the dead were judged according to their works, by the things which were written in the books,*" (Revelation 20:12 NKJV)

At the post office, Mrs. Us found this letter in her post box.

Memo

from: Sonny

to: Mrs. Us

Re: Government, health, freedom, and things to come.

Government

1) A strong and good nation is not produced by strong government, but rather by strong families who know their strong God and produce strong, loving, and caring men and women.

2) Government does not produce wealth nor can it give you good health.

3) Good government protects its citizens, and rewards those who work, produce useful products and share wealth. It punishes those who try to gain wealth by stealing from others, and removes those who wantonly take the lives of others.

Health

1) A nation's health is dependent on the health of its citizens, and the wisdom of its leaders. Remember that the Gift of God brings peace of mind and promotes good health.

2) A healthy and free environment promotes good health. Interesting and challenging work helps to maintain good health. Fear and unstable government increase ill health.

3) A good health plan is one that people want to join, not one that they are *forced* to join.

Freedom

1) Freedom is one of life's greatest treasures; *guard it carefully*. Don't exchange it for promises of free handouts.

2) Your land in the past was known as the land of the free and the home of the brave. Don't let it become the land of the free handouts and the home of slaves to the taxmasters. When needed, use the ballot box to replace those in government who are placing a burden of excess taxes on you to serve their own personal and political goals. Search for men of wisdom, integrity, and stability.

3) Real freedom is based on truth and freedom from oppression. "*And you shall know the truth and the truth shall make you free.*" (John 8:32, NKJV)

Things to come for Mrs. Us

1) A look at your finances seen in Chapter 5 showed that you are continuing to spend far beyond your income. Projections indicate serious economic times in two to four years if you continue your present spending, and crime

continues to increase. Your present course is headed for self-destruction by or before the year 2000 unless you make the right changes now.

2) During difficult times, financial investments and even precious metals often fail to produce security. Real friends are your greatest asset in this life. Best of all you can take them with you to the next life if they have accepted the Gift.

In times of stress infra-structures often fail. Those who have gardens, or can work with friends to produce food and meet their other needs, usually fare better than those who have not prepared.

3) Historical records show that Almighty God blesses the nations that honor Him and punishes the nations that turn away from Him. If you turn to Him soon, you may escape or at least delay coming judgment.

Things to come in the world

1) Just before His death and resurrection, the Chief Designer gathered His disciples together on the mount of Olives, just to the east of Jerusalem. He told them He was coming back to the earth and warned them that before His return, there would be wars and rumors of wars, severe weather, famines, and large earthquakes. Even now you see these events beginning to happen. The ones who have studied the Book and received the Gift will not be surprised. Their hearts will not be worried for they have been told, "*Now when these things begin to happen, look up and lift up your heads, because your redemption draws near.*" Luke 21:28 NKJV

They are also told that before this return to earth (to the Mount of Olives), at a time known only to God, "*For the Lord Himself shall descend from heaven with a shout, with the voice of an archangel, and with the trumpet of God. And the dead in Christ shall rise first. Then we which are alive and remain shall be caught up together with them in the clouds to meet the Lord in the air. And thus we shall always be with the Lord.*" 1 Thessalonians 4: 16,17, NKJV

2) Some 50 years after Christ talked with His disciples on the mount of Olives, the Apostle John wrote some good news and some bad news. In Revelation, he describes events just preceding Christ's return to rule on the earth. First he gives the good news as he describes the scene in Heaven where myriads who have accepted the Gift and have been caught up to heaven are gathered giving thanks and praise to God.

Back on earth we have the bad news where Arch Enemy is active and the four horsemen of the apocalypse—*conquering, war, famine, and death* are released. First there is the *conquering*, the setting up of a one world government. For a while it will appear to be a time of relative peace and safety. Then *war, famine* and *death* will be released for a time of great tribulation. Then there will be a really great earthquake, greater than any since man has been on the earth. The sun will turn dark, the moon red, and comet materials will rain to the earth, similar to what occurred on Jupiter in 1994. Things will be so bad that the mighty men and rich men will seek to hide in caves and in the rocks of the mountains from the wrath of Almighty God.

3) The prophet Zechariah, Chapter 14, describes the end of the tribulation when Christ returns and His feet stand on the Mount of Olives. Then He will subdue the rebelling nations and start His 1000-year rule over the earth.

CHAPTER NOTES

God has provided in the Bible detailed accounts of what has happened to nations, as well as individuals, over the past 6,000 years. The Bible also records details of many events before they happened. Many have been accurately fulfilled while some remain to be fulfilled in the future. The accuracy of the Bible has stood the test of time. It may not agree with some theories of science, but it does agree with the observed facts of science.

God has given us accurate records of the past and information regarding the future so that we might not let shifting political correctness determine our policies. God rewards men and nations for their good deeds, and punishes them for evil. The world is headed for judgment, and we must live in the light of that reality.

Some years ago when giving a lecture at London University, I saw these words on the wall above the platform. "*study the past, prepare for the future.*" If you desire to be prepared for the future, I urge you to:

- study God's instruction book,
- search its ancient pages for hidden wisdom, and
- see how it is still relevent to solve today's problems in the lives of men and nations.

Do this, my friend, and you will be wise and prepared for the future. Remember, **God loves you!** He will reward you with true joy and peace and enable you to show His love and care to those about you.

I have seen the power of God's spirit working in the lives of:

- men and women to make them joyful and kind,
- families binding them together in love,
- churches making them loving and caring,
- communities making them great places to live, and
- nations making them great.

If you and I, and enough of us in this great land, turn to God with all our hearts, the power of His unifying spirit will sweep across our land enabling us to work together instead of against each other. Mrs. Us will regain her health, and we will again be known as, "One nation under God with liberty and justice for all."

[1] Galatians 5:22, NASB
[2] Isaiah 9:6, KJV
[3] 2 Corinthians 5:15, NEB
[4] Luke 9:24, NKJV

Post Script

There is room for all of Mrs. Us's citizens to work together to help her back to health. If you are one who has
been looking for big government to provide a great new
society, I urge you to examine the pages of history and the
record of the past few decades. When you see the failure
of this approach, and how we are turning out new criminals at an alarming rate, I suggest that you become involved in time proven solutions such as are found in the
Bible. If you are one who has taken the time to learn
God's ways, may I suggest that you are needed to instruct
the new generations in God's ways. You can help change
lives that have been shipwrecked by destructive addictions. Be assured that the wisdom of Mrs. Us's advisors
is timeless and much needed in the days ahead.